THE WEALTHY MINDSET:

How To Build Wealth and Avoid the Traps of Riches.

By

Bibian N Okoye

Acknowledgement

I stand in awe and gratitude as I pen down this acknowledgement for my second book. First and foremost, I express my deepest gratitude to God, the Almighty, for His divine guidance and blessings that have been my constant source of inspiration and strength throughout this journey.

To my loving husband, who has been my pillar of support, thank you for your unwavering faith in me and for your endless patience. Your encouragement has been invaluable to me.

To my wonderful children, Gladys, Anthony, Blessing, Esther and Felicita and my in-laws who have been my greatest cheerleaders, thank you for your understanding, love, and for the joy you bring into my life. My thanks also goes to my grandkids who always through their laughs and cries kept me awake and helped me not to sleep off on the work. You all inspire me to be the best version of myself.

A special note of thanks to the Mrs Egwuchukwu Ifensor- (PHD) who meticulously proofread the manuscript and wrote the forward, Your keen eye for detail and your dedication have greatly enhanced the quality of this book.

Your eloquent words have set the perfect tone for the book and have added a unique depth to it.

Lastly, I would like to express my heartfelt appreciation to everyone who has contributed to the production of this book. Your hard work and dedication have not gone unnoticed, and this book would not have been possible without your efforts.

My Thanks also goes to Mr. Solomon Ani for formatting and helping in publishing this book.

Thank you all for being a part of this incredible journey.

DEDICATION

A Journey of Inspiration: Dedicating "THE WEALTHY MINDSET"

Naina Mansukhani: The Guiding Light

Naina Mansukhani, a world-renowned mind coach, has spent over seven transformative years sculpting dynamic entrepreneurs, actors, musicians, students, and professionals into the best versions of themselves. Her unique perspective, drawn from her background as a former lawyer, allows her to connect deeply with individuals, guiding them toward unparalleled success and productivity. Naina's compassion, empathy, and unwavering commitment have been instrumental in shaping my mindset and driving me forward.

>> Learn more about Naina Mansukhani on her website: nainamindworks.com

I also dedicate this book to my son, Anthony Chukwuemeka Okoye, whose unwavering support, and encouragement have been instrumental in bringing this book to life.

Anthony Chukwuemeka Okoye is a remarkable individual known for his dedication to personal growth, philanthropy, and positive impact. His unwavering support and encouragement have left an impression on those fortunate enough to know him. Whether through mentorship, community service, or entrepreneurial endeavors, Anthony exemplifies the values of resilience, kindness, and ambition.

Currently he is running a foundation known as Tony Chukwuemeka foundation where he helps those less privileged with different gifts.

Other Motivational Speakers: A Symphony of Inspiration

Beyond Naina, and Chukwuemeka, Afreen, and Andy, there are countless other motivational speakers who have played pivotal roles in my journey. Their words, wisdom, and encouragement have fuelled my determination. Each speaker, like a unique instrument in an orchestra, contributes to the symphony of inspiration that resonates within me.

In dedicating "THE WEALTHY MINDSET," I honour these remarkable individuals who have shaped my path. Their compassion, care, and unwavering belief in human potential have been my guiding stars. May their influence continue to ripple through the lives of others, just as it has in mine.

Mission Statement

I want to write this book to inspire and motivate you to adopt a healthy attitude towards wealth. Many people pursue wealth to extremes, sometimes with tragic consequences like death, imprisonment, or family disgrace. Even those who succeed often struggle with how to manage their wealth.

Forward

Introducing "The Wealthy Mindset: How to Build Wealth and Avoid the Traps of Riches" by Bibian N. Okoye

This book takes you on a transformative journey into the world of wealth creation, protection, management, and enjoyment. In a world where success is often equated with wealth, it's easy to believe that accumulating money is the ultimate goal in life. However, this book inspires you to cultivate the right mindset towards wealth through insightful guidance and practical advice.

Bibian delves into the intricacies of the human mind, outlining the principles and skills that distinguish wealth accumulation from lifelong prosperity. She advocates for a healthy attitude towards creating, maintaining, and managing wealth. Drawing from her personal experiences and extensive research, the author provides a comprehensive guide and practical strategies to help you develop a mindset that not only builds wealth but also ensures its longevity.

"The Wealthy Mindset" covers various aspects, including setting and achieving financial goals, growing wealth with happiness, protecting wealth and assets, guilt-free enjoyment of wealth, and key principles for wealth creation. The book is inspiring, encouraging, and motivating, equipping you with the knowledge and skills necessary for wise wealth-building, maintenance, and enjoyment. It also addresses common misconceptions about personal finance and explores the connection between wealth mindsets, relationships, and management.

Bibian's passion to empower readers to live abundantly shines through every page of this valuable resource. She emphasizes that true financial success extends beyond the amount of money in your bank account, highlighting the importance of relationships, impact, and leaving a lasting legacy.

If you are ready to shift your mindset from chasing money to building, protecting, managing, and enjoying real wealth without worries, "The Wealthy Mindset" is the book for you. Dive into its pages, absorb the content, and embark on a journey towards a life of abundance and fulfilment.

Egwuchukwu Ifensor Ike-Okafor _PhD_

TABLE OF CONTENT

INTRODUCTION

Did you know that about 80% of lottery winners end up broke within five years? Or that many celebrities, athletes, and entrepreneurs who achieve fame and fortune end up unhappy, addicted, or bankrupt? What makes some people wealthy and others poor, even when they have the same amount of money? The answer is simple: it is their mindset.

If you are like most people, you probably have some financial goals you want to achieve. Maybe you want to pay off your debt, save for retirement, buy a house, or travel the world. But no matter how hard you work, how much you earn, or how much you save, you never get closer to your dreams. You feel stuck, frustrated, and hopeless. You wonder why money is so hard to make, keep, and grow. You blame the economy, the government, the taxes, or the system. You think that wealth is reserved for the lucky few who were born with a silver spoon in their mouth or who have some special talent, skill, or secret.

But what if I told you that there is a better way? A way that can help you create, manage, and multiply your wealth without sacrificing your happiness, health, or integrity. A way that can help you achieve financial freedom, security, and abundance, no matter what your background, education, or income level. A way that can help you avoid the common pitfalls and traps that many rich people fall into, such as greed, envy, arrogance, or complacency. A way that can help you live a rich and fulfilling life, not only in terms of money but also in terms of relationships, experiences, and impact. That way is the wealthy mindset.

In this book, you will learn what the wealthy mindset is and how it differs from the poor mindset or the rich mindset. You will discover the principles, habits, and skills that can help you develop and cultivate a wealthy mindset, regardless of your current financial situation. You will also learn how to avoid the common mistakes and challenges that many people face when they try to build wealth or deal with riches. By the end of this book, you will be able to:

a) Set and achieve your financial goals with clarity, confidence, and ease.

b) Manage your money wisely and efficiently, without stress or worry.

c) Grow your wealth exponentially by leveraging the power of compounding, investing, and entrepreneurship.

d) Protect your wealth from inflation, taxes, lawsuits, or scams.

e) Enjoy your wealth without guilt, fear, or regret.

f) Share your wealth generously and wisely with your family, friends, and causes that matter to you.

My name is Bibian N. Okoye, and I am a certified financial planner, coach, and speaker. I have helped thousands of people from all walks of life to achieve their financial goals and dreams. I have also experienced firsthand the highs and lows of wealth and riches. I grew up in a poor family, where money was always scarce and stressful. I worked hard to get a good education, an excellent job, and a good income.

I thought that money would solve all my problems and make me happy. But I was wrong. I became addicted to spending and impressing others. I accumulated thousands of debts, stress, and unhappiness. I almost lost everything: my family, my health, and my sanity. That is when I realized that I needed to change my mindset and my habits. I started to study and apply the principles and practices of the wealthy mindset. I learned how to save, invest, and grow my money. I learned how to manage, protect, and enjoy my money. I learned how to share, donate, and have influence with my money. And I learned how to be happy, grateful, and fulfilled with my money. That is why I decided to write this book: to share with you that I have learned and to help you achieve the same results.

So, are you ready to transform your financial life and your whole life with the wealthy mindset? Are you ready to build wealth and avoid the traps of riches? Are you ready to live a rich and fulfilling life, not only in terms of money but also in terms of relationships, experiences, and impact? If you are, then I invite you to join me on this journey. Let us get started!

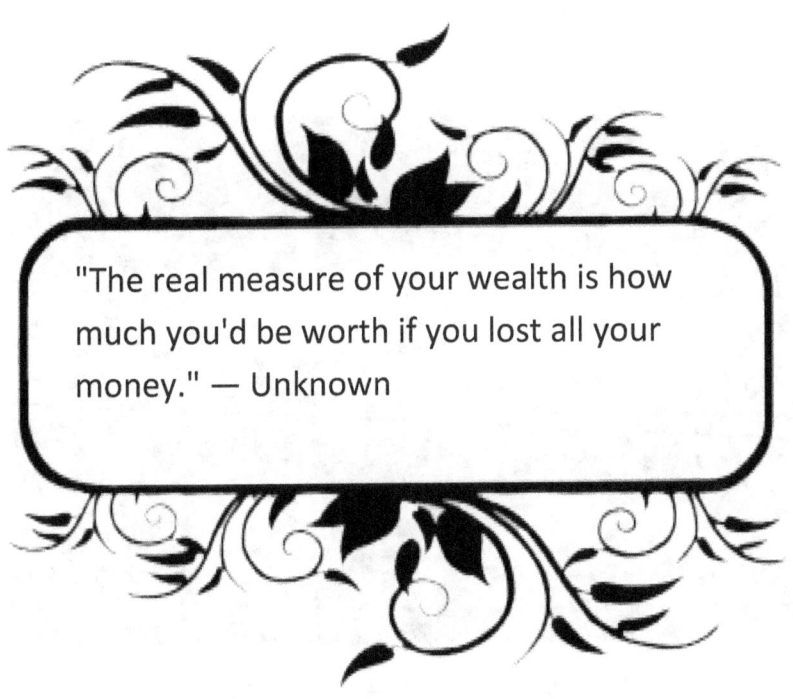

"The real measure of your wealth is how much you'd be worth if you lost all your money." — Unknown

CHAPTER ONE

Start Your Journey

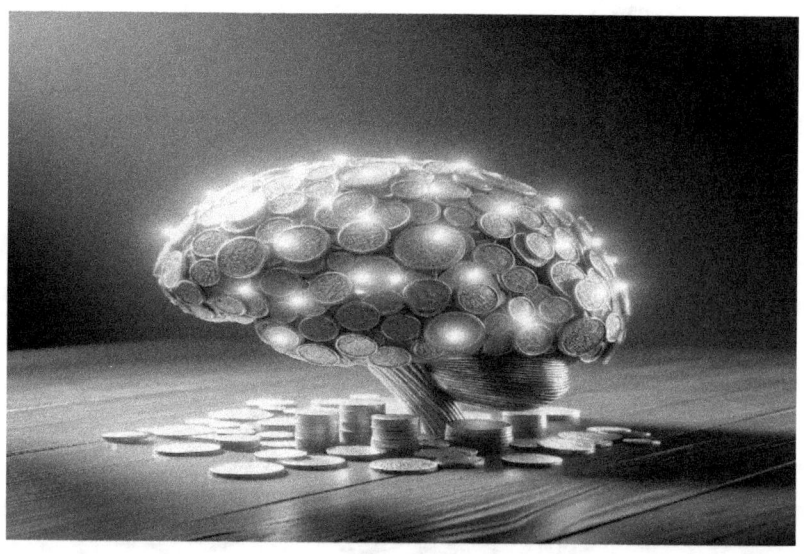

In this chapter you would read and understand the instructions of the things to help you flow in this journey. The things you should read and understand are understanding what the financial goals are and why they are important for personal and professional success. Some of examples of common financial goals are, saving for retirement, paying off debt, buying a house, or starting a business. You can also see some of the benefits of setting and achieving financial goals, such as financial security, peace of mind, and personal satisfaction.

Some of the steps involved in setting and achieving these financial goals can also be seen in these subheadings.

Assess your current financial situation: Analyse your income, expenses, assets, liabilities, and net worth. Identify your strengths and weaknesses, and areas where you can improve. Some of the tools such as budgeting apps, financial calculators, or spreadsheets to help these steps. The first goal is.

Defining your specific and realistic financial goals: Based on your financial situation and your personal preferences, decide what you want to achieve and by when. Make sure your goals are SMART, which stands for Specific, Measurable, Attainable, Relevant, and Time-bound. For example, instead of saying "I want to save more money", you can say "I want to save $10,000 for a down payment on a house in two years".

Create a plan of action: Outline the strategies and actions you will take to reach your financial goals. For example, you can create a budget, reduce your expenses, increase your income, save, and invest your money, or seek professional advice. You can also break down your goals into smaller and manageable milestones and track your progress regularly.

Review and adjust your plan as needed: Evaluate your performance and results periodically and celebrate your achievements. If you encounter any challenges or changes in your circumstances, be flexible and adaptable, and modify your plan accordingly. You can also seek feedback and support from others, such as family, friends, mentors, or financial experts.

I recommend some books and movies that can help you develop a wealthy mindset. A wealthy mindset is a set of beliefs, habits, and behaviours that can help you achieve your financial goals and live a fulfilling life.

According to the web search results from Bing, some of the best books and movies for wealthy mindset are:

Mindset: The New Psychology of Success by Carol Dweck. This book is based on decades of research on how people's mindsets affect their performance and success. It shows how you can adopt a growth mindset that embraces challenges, learns from failures, and seeks improvement.

The Wolf of Wall Street (2013). This movie is based on the true story of Jordan Belfort, who rose from a penny stockbroker to a wealthy and notorious Wall Street trader. It depicts his lavish and reckless lifestyle, as well as his downfall due to fraud and corruption.

The Power of Broke by Daymond John. This book is written by the founder of FUBU and a Shark Tank investor, who started his clothing brand with a $40 budget. It shows how having limited resources can be an advantage, and how you can use your creativity, passion, and hustle to succeed.

The Big Short (2015). This movie is based on the book by Michael Lewis, who chronicled the 2008 financial crisis and the people who predicted and profited from it. It exposes the flaws and corruption of the mortgage market, and the consequences of the collapse.

The Richest Man in Babylon by George Clason. This book is a classic that teaches the timeless principles of wealth creation and preservation. It uses stories and parables from ancient Babylon to illustrate the importance of saving, investing, and avoiding debt.

These are some of the books and movies that I recommend for wealthy mindset, but there are many more. You can find more suggestions by using the related searches from Bing, such as "best books on wealth creation" or "best movies about money and success". I hope you enjoy them and learn something valuable from them.

FINANCIAL GOALS AND THEIR IMPORTANCE

Financial goals are measuring sticks that apply to any area of your money management skills that you're looking to improve. They can be short-term or long-term, personal or professional, specific or general. For example, some common financial goals are saving for retirement, paying off debt, buying a house, or starting a business.

The importance of setting financial goals is that they can help you:

Focus and create a practical plan of action. Having a clear and compelling goal can motivate you to take steps toward achieving it, such as creating a budget, a savings plan, an investment strategy, or an estate plan. Having a goal can also help you prioritize your spending and saving habits and avoid unnecessary or impulsive purchases.

Monitor your progress and adjustments: having a goal also means having a timeline and a target to reach. You can track your performance and compare it with your expectations and see if you are on track or need to make changes. You can also celebrate your achievements and reward yourself for your efforts.

Improve your financial well-being and security: Having a goal can help you improve your financial situation and prepare for the future. You can reduce your debt, increase your income, build your wealth, and achieve your dreams. You can also protect yourself and your loved ones from financial risks, such as inflation, taxes, lawsuits, or scams.

SOME OF THE TIPS OR RESOURCES ON SETTING FINANCIAL GOALS ARE

Use the SMART goal framework. SMART stands for specific, measurable, achievable, relevant, and time bound. This framework can help you set realistic and clear financial goals, monitor your progress, and stay motivated1.

Consult a financial professional; A financial advisor, planner, or coach can help you assess your current financial situation, identify your financial goals and values, and create a personalized plan to achieve them. They can also provide you with guidance, support, and accountability along the way.

Use online tools and apps; There are various online tools and apps that can help you set and reach your financial goals, such as budgeting tools, automated saving apps, online banking tools, financial calculators, and goal-tracking apps. You can use these resources to manage your money, save and invest, monitor your transactions and accounts, and track your performance .

Join a financial community; A financial community is a group of people who share similar financial goals, interests, or challenges, and who support each other in their financial journeys. You can join a financial community online or offline, such as a blog, a podcast, a forum, a club, or a class. You can learn from others' experiences, insights, and tips, and also share your own too.

ONLINE COMMUNITY FOR PERSONAL FINANCE

Personal finance:

One way to find an online community for personal finance is to use a web search engine, such as Bing, Chrome or Edge and type in keywords related to your interests, goals, or challenges. For example, you can search for "online community for personal finance", "online forum for budgeting", or "online group for investing". You can also use filters or advanced search options to narrow down your results by date, relevance, or popularity.

Another way to find an online community for personal finance is to use the web search results that I have provided for you. I have used the query "online community for personal finance" and found some relevant and popular websites that offer various online platforms and groups for people who want to improve their money management skills. Here are some of the websites that you can check out:

CNBC: This website has an article that lists five online personal finance communities that can help you get better with money. The article describes the features, benefits, and topics of each community, such as Reddit, Financial Common Cents, Bravely, The Bogleheads Forum, and Your Money and Your Life1.

Oberlo: This website has a blog post that ranks the 11 best personal finance blogs in 2023. The blog post explains the purpose, content, and audience of each blog, such as NerdWallet, Good Financial Cents, The Balance, Mint, and The Simple Dollar.

U.S. News: This website has an article that recommends 12 free online personal finance courses that you can take to learn more about budgeting, saving, investing, and more.

The article provides the names, descriptions, and links of each course, such as Personal Finance 101, Financial Planning for Young Adults, Investing for Beginners, and Money Essentials.

Family Coach to Wealth: Financial planning for kids

Some Possible Topics or Questions to Ask in A Personal Finance Community Are:

How do you budget your income and expenses? What tools or methods do you use?

What are your short-term and long-term financial goals? How are you working towards them?

What are some of the best ways to save money on everyday expenses, such as groceries, utilities, or transportation?

What are some of the best ways to earn extra income, such as side hustles, passive income, or online opportunities?

How do you manage your debt, such as credit cards, student loans, or mortgages? What strategies or tips do you have to pay off debt faster or reduce interest rates?

How do you invest your money, such as stocks, bonds, mutual funds, or ETFs? What are some of the best resources or platforms to learn about investing?

How do you plan for retirement, such as saving, investing, or choosing a retirement account?

How much do you need to retire comfortably?

How do you protect your wealth, such as insurance, estate planning, or tax optimization?

What are some of the common risks or challenges that you face or anticipate?

How do you balance your financial needs and wants, such as spending, saving, or giving?

How do you deal with financial stress or anxiety?

How do you improve your financial literacy, such as reading books, blogs, podcasts, or courses?

What are some of the best personal finance books or podcasts that you recommend?

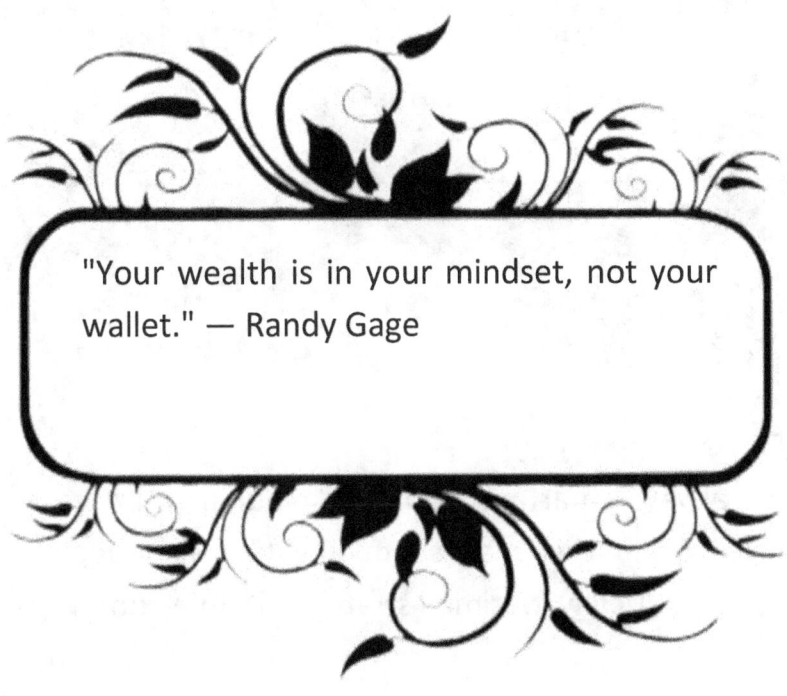

"Your wealth is in your mindset, not your wallet." — Randy Gage

CHAPTER TWO

SOME MYTHS AND MISTAKES

Some Common Mistakes or Myths About Personal Finance

It's always smartest to pay off your high-interest debt first. While this may seem like the most logical and mathematically optimal strategy, it may not work for everyone. Some people may benefit from paying off their smaller debts first, as this can provide them with a psychological boost and motivation to keep going. This is known as the snowball method, and it can help you reduce your debt faster and easier than the avalanche method, which focuses on the highest interest rate debt first.

It's okay to just make the credit card minimum payments. This is a dangerous trap that can keep you in debt for years and cost you a lot of money in interest. Credit card companies set the minimum payments low to encourage you to pay more interest over time. If you only pay the minimum, you will barely make a dent in your principal balance, and it will take you much longer to pay off your debt. For example, if you have $10,000 of credit card debt with a 15% APR and a 2% minimum payment, it will take you 35 years and $15,000 in interest to pay it off. However, if you pay $250 per month, you will pay it off in 6.5 years and $5,700 in interest.

Carrying a credit card balance is good for my credit score. This is a common misconception that can hurt your credit score and your wallet. Carrying a balance on your credit card does not improve your credit score, but it does increase your credit utilization ratio, which is the percentage of your available credit that you use. A high credit utilization ratio can lower your credit score, as it indicates that you are a risky borrower. It also means that you are paying interest on your balance, which can add up over time. The best way to use your credit card is to pay off your balance in full every month and keep your credit utilization ratio below 30 percent.

I don't earn enough to save. This is a common excuse that many people use to avoid saving money. However, saving money is not about how much you earn, but how much you spend and save. Even if you have a low income, you can still save money by cutting your expenses, finding ways to increase your income, and setting aside a portion of your money for savings. You can also use online tools and apps to help you budget, automate your savings, and track your progress. Saving money is important for your financial security and well-being, and it can help you achieve your short-term and long-term goals.

More income means more wealth. This is another myth that can prevent you from building wealth and achieving financial freedom. While having a high income can help you save and invest more money, it does not guarantee that you will be wealthy. Wealth is not measured by how much you earn, but by how much you keep and grow. Many people who earn a lot of money also spend a lot of money, and end up living paycheck to paycheck or in debt. To build wealth, you need to live below your means, save and invest your money wisely, and avoid lifestyle inflation, which is the tendency to increase your spending as your income rises.

Based on the web search results, here are some of the steps to set and achieve financial goals:

Figure out what matters to you; Consider everything, from the practical and pressing to the whimsical and distant and write down your financial goals. They can be short-term, mid-term, or long-term, depending on when you want to achieve them.

Make your goals SMART, SMART stands for specific, measurable, achievable, relevant, and time bound. This framework can help you make your goals realistic and clear and track your progress and results.

Create a budget and a plan; A budget is a tool that helps you manage your income and expenses and allocate your money to your needs and wants. A plan is a strategy that helps you achieve your goals, such as saving, investing, or paying off debt. You can use online tools or apps, or consult a financial professional, to help you create and follow your budget and plan1234.

Prioritize your goals and take action; You may have multiple goals, but you can't achieve them all at once. You need to prioritize your goals based on their importance, urgency, and difficulty, and focus on the ones that matter most to you. You also need to take action and implement your plan, such as setting up automatic transfers, cutting expenses, or increasing income123.

Monitor your progress and make adjustments; You should regularly review your goals and your performance and see if you are on track or need to make changes. You should also celebrate your achievements and reward yourself for your efforts. You can also learn from your mistakes and challenges and seek help or advice if needed123.

Enjoy your wealth and share it with others. Once you achieve your goals, you should enjoy the benefits and rewards of your hard work, such as buying a house, travelling, or retiring. You should also share your wealth with others who are less fortunate or in need, and support causes or organizations that you care about. This can help you create a positive impact and a legacy, and make you feel more fulfilled and connected.

How to stay motivated and accountable when working towards financial goals

Working towards your financial goals can be challenging and rewarding, but also requires motivation and accountability. Based on the web search results, here are some tips on how to stay motivated and accountable when working towards your financial goals:

Focus on your "why"; Your "why" is the reason or purpose behind your financial goals, and it can help you stay motivated and inspired. Think about what you want to achieve with your money, and how it aligns with your values, passions, and dreams. You can also create visual reminders of your "why", such as pictures, quotes, or charts, and keep them in a place where you can see them every day.

Break down your goals into smaller steps. Your financial goals may seem overwhelming or daunting, especially if they are long-term or complex. To make them more manageable and achievable, you can break them down into smaller and specific steps and assign them a timeline and a target. For example, if your goal is to save $10,000 in a year, you can break it down into monthly or weekly savings goals and track your progress123.

Celebrate your milestones and achievements. As you work towards your financial goals, you should also acknowledge and reward yourself for your efforts and accomplishments. Celebrating your milestones and achievements can boost your confidence and motivation and reinforce your positive habits. You can also share your success with others who support you and get feedback and encouragement.

Seek support and accountability. Working towards your financial goals can be easier and more fun if you have someone or a group of people who can help you stay on track and accountable. You can find a friend, a family member, a mentor, or a coach who can check in with you regularly, offer advice and guidance, and hold you responsible for your actions. You can also join an online or offline community of people who share similar financial goals, interests, or challenges, and learn from their experiences, insights, and tips123.

Review your goals and adjust them as needed. Your financial goals are not set in stone, and they may change over time as your circumstances, preferences, or opportunities change. You should review your goals periodically and evaluate your performance and results. You should also be flexible and adaptable and adjust your goals or plans as needed. You should also learn from your mistakes and setbacks and seek help or advice if needed123.

These are some of the tips on how to stay motivated and accountable when working towards your financial goals. However, you should also do your own research, seek professional advice, and make informed decisions based on your specific needs and circumstances.

Common Distractions or Temptations That Can Derail Financial Goals

Some common distractions or temptations that can derail your financial goals are:

Impulsive spending. This is when you buy things that you don't need or can't afford, without thinking or planning. Impulsive spending can make you miss your budget, savings, or investment targets, and increase your debt and interest payments. To avoid impulsive spending, you should have a clear and realistic budget, and stick to it. You should also avoid using your credit card for unnecessary purchases and pay off your balance in full every month. You should also ask yourself if you really need or want something before you buy it and think about how it will add value or happiness to your life.

Chasing high returns. This is when you invest your money in risky or speculative assets, hoping to get higher returns than the market average. Chasing high returns can expose you to more volatility, losses, and fees, and make you deviate from your original investment strategy and goals. To avoid chasing high returns, you should have a clear and consistent investment plan, based on your risk tolerance, time horizon, and objectives. You should also diversify your portfolio across different asset classes, sectors, and regions, and rebalance it periodically. You should also avoid following the crowd or the media hype and do your own research and analysis.

Lifestyle inflation. This is when you increase your spending as your income rises and adjust your lifestyle to a higher standard of living. Lifestyle inflation can prevent you from saving and investing enough money for your future goals, such as retirement, education, or travel. It can also make you more vulnerable to financial shock, such as job loss, illness, or market downturns. To avoid lifestyle inflation, you should live below your means, and save and invest a portion of your income for your long-term goals. You should also avoid comparing yourself with others or feeling pressured to keep up with the Joneses. You should also be grateful for what you have and enjoy your wealth moderately and mindfully.

Procrastination. This is when you delay or postpone acting on your financial goals, such as creating a budget, saving money, or investing. Procrastination can make you miss out on opportunities, benefits, and compounding effects, and make your goals harder to achieve. To avoid procrastination, you should break down your goals into smaller and specific steps and assign them a deadline and a reward. You should also track your progress and celebrate your achievements. You should also seek support and accountability from others, such as a friend, a family member, or a financial professional 124.

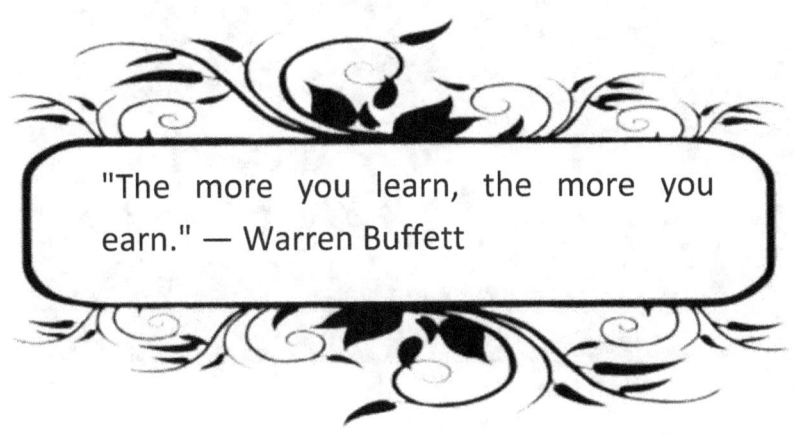

"The more you learn, the more you earn." — Warren Buffett

CHAPTER THREE

PEER PRESSURE OR SOCIAL EXPECTATIONS TO MONEY

Peer pressure or social expectations can be a challenge when it comes to money, as they can influence you to spend more than you can afford, or on things that you don't need or want. However, there are some ways to deal with peer pressure or social expectations and manage your money wisely. Based on the web search results, here are some tips on how to deal with peer pressure or social expectations when it comes to money:

Let your budget be your guide. A budget is a plan that helps you track your income and expenses and allocate your money to your needs and wants. A budget can help you control your spending, save money, and achieve your financial goals. You can use online tools or apps to help you create and manage your budget, such as Mint, YNAB, or Pocketbook. You should review your budget regularly and adjust it as needed.

Establish financial boundaries with your friends. Setting boundaries is important in any relationship for building trust and mutual understanding. You should communicate your financial goals and values to your friends and let them know what you can and cannot afford to do. You should also respect their financial choices and avoid judging or criticizing them. You can also suggest alternative activities that are more affordable or free, such as going for a walk, watching a movie, or playing a game.

Remember who's in control. You are the only one who can decide how to spend your money, and you should not let others pressure or influence you to do something that you are not comfortable with. You should also avoid comparing yourself with others or feeling pressured to keep up with the Joneses. You should focus on your own financial situation and goals, and what makes you happy and satisfied. You should also be grateful for what you have and enjoy your wealth moderately and mindfully132.

Seek support and accountability. Working towards your financial goals can be easier and more fun if you have someone or a group of people who can help you stay on track and accountable. You can find a friend, a family member, a mentor, or a coach who can check in with you regularly, offer advice and guidance, and hold you responsible for your actions. You can also join an online or offline community of people who share similar financial goals, interests, or challenges, and learn from their experiences, insights, and tips. Some examples of online personal finance communities are Reddit, Financial Common Cents, Bravely, The Bogleheads Forum, and Your Money and Your Life.

These are some of the tips on how to deal with peer pressure or social expectations when it comes to money. However, you should also do your own research, seek professional advice, and make informed decisions based on your specific needs and circumstances.

Courses or Workshops on Personal Finance and Communication Skills

PERSONAL FINANCE
Here are some of the options that you can consider:

Effective Communication and Interpersonal Skills. This is a live online short course offered by City, University of London. It helps you to improve your communication skills by noticing and responding to the non-verbal, subconscious cues of others. It also strengthens your communication across a variety of settings through a broad range of tools and techniques. The course is delivered over 10 weekly evening classes.

Workshops and Training from The Money Charity. These are workshops and webinars offered by The Money Charity, a UK-based organisation that aims to help people improve their money management skills. They cover topics such as budgeting, saving, investing, and debt management. They are available for people of all ages and stages of life and can be delivered face-to-face or virtually. The prices vary depending on the type and length of the workshop or webinar.

Five online courses to improve your personal finance skills. This is a blog post by Future Learn, an online learning platform that offers courses from top universities and industry leaders. The blog post lists five of the best personal finance courses that you can take on Future Learn, such as Personal Finance Fundamentals, Managing My Money, and Financial Planning for Young Adults. The courses are free to join, but you can also upgrade to get a certificate or unlimited access.

Best Personal Finance Courses & Certificates Online. This is a collection of personal finance courses offered by Coursera, another online learning platform that partners with leading universities and organisations. The courses cover various aspects of personal finance, such as financial literacy, financial planning, financial markets, and financial independence. The courses are self-paced and flexible, and you can also earn a certificate or a degree upon completion. The prices vary depending on the course and the credential.

The Skills Toolkit. This is a website by the National Careers Service, a UK government agency that provides information and advice on careers, skills, and training. The website offers a range of free online courses that can help you improve your skills and boost your employability. Some of the courses are related to personal finance and communication skills, such as Business and Finance Fundamentals, Effective Communication and Interpersonal Skills, and Professional Development5.

I hope these recommendations can help you find a course or workshop that suits your needs and preferences. ☐.

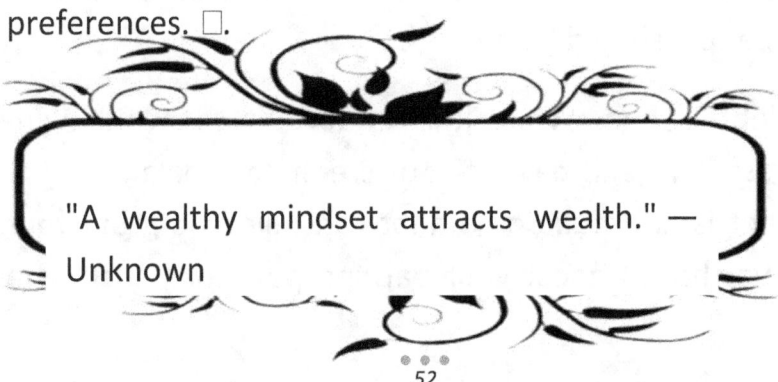

"A wealthy mindset attracts wealth." — Unknown

FINANCIAL PLANNING
Setting up a better future

Current Financial Situation - determine your current financial situation with regard to income, savings, living expenses, and debts.

Develop Financial Goals - periodically analyze your financial values and goals. This involves identifying how you feel about money and why.

Alternative Courses of Action - Continue the same course of action. Expand the current situation. Change the current situation.

Evaluate Alternatives - evaluate courses of action, considering your life situation, personal values, and current economic conditions.

Implement a Financial Action Plan - as you achieve your immediate or short-term goals, the goals next in priority will come into focus.

Revise Your Plan - this process does not end when you take a particular action. You need to regularly assess your financial decisions.

Some common misconceptions about personal finance that people should be aware of

All debt is bad. While it is important to avoid high-interest debt and pay off your credit card balances, not all debt is harmful. Some debt can help you grow your net worth and boost your earning potential, such as a mortgage, a student loan, or a business loan. These types of debt can also have tax benefits and lower interest rates. The key is to manage your debt wisely and have a plan to pay it off.

It is normal to have a lot of debt. While many people have some form of debt, such as a car loan, a student loan, or a mortgage, having too much debt can hurt your financial future. Having a lot of debt can prevent you from saving and investing enough for your goals, such as retirement, education, or travel. It can also make you more vulnerable to financial shock, such as job loss, illness, or market downturns. The best way to avoid or reduce debt is to live below your means, save and invest a portion of your income, and avoid lifestyle inflation123.

Slashing expenses is the only way to save more money and build wealth. While cutting your expenses can help you save money and achieve your financial goals, it is not the only way. You can also increase your income by finding ways to earn extra money, such as side hustles, passive income, or online opportunities. You can also invest your money wisely and take advantage of compound interest, which can help you grow your wealth over time. The best way to save more money and build wealth is to have a balanced and realistic budget and stick to it124.

Buying a new car is a good investment. While buying a new car can be tempting, it is not a good investment. A new car loses a lot of its value as soon as you drive it off the lot, and it continues to depreciate over time. A new car also costs more to buy, insure, and maintain than a used car. Unless you need a new car for your work or safety, it is better to buy a reliable and fuel-efficient used car or use public transportation or car-sharing services. This can help you save money and avoid taking on more debt.

More income means more wealth. While having a high income can help you save and invest more money, it does not guarantee that you will be wealthy. Wealth is not measured by how much you earn, but by how much you keep and grow. Many people who earn a lot of money also spend a lot of money and end up living paycheck to paycheck or in debt. To build wealth, you need to live below your means, save and invest a portion of your income, and avoid lifestyle inflation.

These are some of the common misconceptions about personal finance that people should be aware of.

However, you should also do your own research, seek professional advice, and make informed decisions based on your specific needs and circumstances □.

Writing a good essay/article can also yield you some wealth. Before you start follow the instructions below.

How to write a good essay (Articles)

Plan your essay before you start writing. This will help you to organize your thoughts, identify the main points, and create a clear structure for your essay. You can use different methods to plan your essay, such as brainstorming, mind mapping, outlining, or writing a thesis statement123.

Have a clear introduction, body, and conclusion. Your introduction should introduce the topic, provide some background information, and state your main argument or thesis. Your body paragraphs should each focus on one aspect of your argument and provide evidence and analysis to support it. Your conclusion should summarize your main points, restate your thesis, and provide some implications or recommendations124.

Use relevant and reliable sources to support your argument. You should use a variety of sources, such as books, articles, websites, or reports, to find information and evidence for your essay. You should also evaluate the credibility and accuracy of your sources and cite them properly according to the referencing style required by your instructor or institution125.

Write in a clear, concise, and formal style. You should use appropriate vocabulary, grammar, and punctuation to communicate your ideas effectively. You should also avoid using slang, jargon, or colloquialisms, and use transitions and connectors to link your sentences and paragraphs. You should also proofread and edit your essay for any errors or mistakes before submitting it123.

Review and revise your essay as needed. You should always check your essay against the essay question or title, and make sure that you have answered it fully and accurately. You should also seek feedback from others, such as your peers, tutors, or mentors, and incorporate their suggestions and comments into your essay. You should also read your essay aloud, or use a text-to-speech tool, to hear how it sounds and spot any issues123.

I hope these tips help you to write a good essay/articles. If you need more help, feel free to contact me at or support@familycoachtowealth.com

Citation

Citing sources properly is essential in academic writing, as it helps you avoid plagiarism and gives credit to the original authors of the information you use. There are different ways to cite sources properly, depending on the citation style you are required to follow. Some of the most common citation styles are:

APA style: This style is widely used in the social sciences and beyond. It uses parenthetical in-text citations that include the author's surname and the year of publication, followed by a page number if applicable. For example: (Smith, 2013, p. 42). The full details of the sources are listed in a reference list at the end of the paper, arranged alphabetically by the author's surname. For example: Smith, J. (2013). Statistical analysis. 2nd ed. London: Penguin. You can use the free Scriber Citation Generator1 to create accurate APA citations.

MLA style: This style is common in the humanities. It uses parenthetical in-text citations that include the author's surname and the page number where the information was found. For example: (Smith 42). The full details of the sources are listed in a works cited list at the end of the paper, arranged alphabetically by the author's surname. For example: Smith, John. Statistical Analysis. 2nd ed., Penguin, 2013. You can use the free Scribbr Citation Generator2 to create accurate MLA citations.

Chicago style: This style consists of two systems: Chicago notes and bibliography, common in the humanities, and Chicago author-date, used in the (social) sciences. The notes and bibliography system uses footnotes or endnotes to cite sources, followed by a bibliography at the end of the paper. The author-date system uses parenthetical in-text citations that include the author's surname and the year of publication, followed by a reference list at the end of the paper. You can use the free Scribbr Citation Generator1 to create accurate Chicago citations.

There are many other citation styles for different disciplines, such as Harvard, Vancouver, MHRA, OSCOLA, and more. You can find more information about these styles and how to cite sources properly by reading the articles from Scribbr132 or Plagiarism.org4. You can also use the Scribbr Plagiarism Checker to make sure you have cited all your sources correctly and avoid plagiarism. I hope this helps you with your citation questions. If you need more assistance, feel free to ask me. □

How to avoid credit card debt

Credit card debt is a common problem that can affect your financial well-being and future goals. Credit card debt can accumulate when you spend more than you can afford to pay back, or when you only make the minimum payments on your balance. Credit card debt can also incur high interest charges, fees, and penalties, which can make it harder to pay off. However, there are some ways to avoid credit card debt and use credit responsibly. Based on the web search results, here are some tips on how to avoid credit card debt:

Pay off your entire balance each month. This is the best way to avoid interest charges and fees, and to keep your credit utilization ratio low. Your credit utilization ratio is the percentage of your available credit that you use, and it affects your credit score. A low credit utilization ratio indicates that you are a responsible borrower and can improve your credit score123.

Only use your credit card for essential purchases. If you only use your credit card for things you need, such as groceries, utilities, or transportation, you are less likely to overspend and rack up unnecessary debt. You should also avoid using your credit card for impulse purchases, such as clothes, gadgets, or entertainment, that you can't afford or don't need. You should also avoid using your credit card for cash advances, such as ATM withdrawals or gambling, as these usually incur higher interest rates and fees124.

Make a budget and stick to it. A budget is a plan that helps you track your income and expenses and allocate your money to your needs and wants. A budget can help you control your spending, save money, and achieve your financial goals. You can use online tools or apps to help you create and manage your budget, such as Mint, YNAB, or Pocketbook. You should review your budget regularly and adjust it as needed124.

Reduce your credit limit and number of credit cards. Your credit limit is the maximum amount of money that you can borrow on your credit card. Your number of credit cards is the total number of credit accounts that you have. Reducing your credit limit and number of credit cards can help you avoid overspending and accumulating debt, as well as simplify your payments and statements. You can contact your credit card issuer and request to lower your credit limit or close your credit card account. However, you should be careful not to lower your credit limit or close your credit card account too much or too often, as this can also affect your credit score negatively123.

Seek help if you are struggling with credit card debt. If you feel that your credit card debt is out of control, you should not ignore it or avoid it, as this can make the situation worse. You should contact your credit card issuer and explain your situation, and see if they can offer you any assistance, such as a lower interest rate, a payment plan, or a hardship program. You can also seek help from a financial counsellor, who can provide you with free and confidential advice and support on how to manage your debt and improve your financial situation. You can find a financial counsellor near you on the National Debt Helpline website124.

These are some of the tips on how to avoid credit card debt. However, you should also do your own research, seek professional advice, and make informed decisions based on your specific needs and circumstances.

CHAPTER FOUR

MANAGING FINANCES EFFECTIVELY AND HAPPILY

Managing finances effectively and happily is a skill that can benefit anyone, regardless of their income level, age, or background. It can help you achieve your short-term and long-term goals, reduce your stress and anxiety, and improve your quality of life. However, many people struggle with managing their finances, either because they lack the knowledge, the motivation, or the discipline to do so. In this essay, I will discuss some of the steps and strategies that can help you manage your finances effectively and happily.

The first step to managing your finances effectively and happily is to have a clear and realistic picture of your current financial situation. This means that you need to gather all the information about your income, expenses, assets, liabilities, and net worth, and organize them in a way that makes sense to you. You can use tools such as budgeting apps, financial calculators, or spreadsheets to help you with this step. By doing this, you will be able to see where your money is coming from and where it is going, identify your strengths and weaknesses, and find areas where you can improve.

The second step to managing your finances effectively and happily is to define your specific and measurable financial goals. These are the things that you want to achieve with your money, such as saving for retirement, paying off debt, buying a house, or starting a business. You should make sure that your goals are SMART, which stands for Specific, Measurable, Attainable, Relevant, and Time-bound. For example, instead of saying "I want to save more money", you can say "I want to save $10,000 for a down payment on a house in two years". By setting SMART goals, you will be able to track your progress, stay motivated, and celebrate your achievements.

The third step to managing your finances effectively and happily is to create a plan of action that outlines the strategies and actions that you will take to reach your financial goals. For example, you can create a budget that allocates your income to your needs, wants, and savings, and stick to it. You can also reduce your expenses by cutting unnecessary costs, finding cheaper alternatives, or negotiating better deals. You can also increase your income by asking for a raise, finding a side hustle, or investing your money wisely. You can also seek professional advice from financial planners, debt counsellors, or credit experts, if you need help with your plan.

The fourth step to managing your finances effectively and happily is to review and adjust your plan as needed. You should evaluate your performance and results periodically and compare them with your goals and expectations. You should also be flexible and adaptable to any changes or challenges that may arise in your circumstances, such as income loss, unexpected expenses, or emergencies. You should also seek feedback and support from others, such as family, friends, mentors, or online communities, who can offer you advice, encouragement, or accountability.

The fifth and final step to managing your finances effectively and happily is to enjoy the process and the outcome. You should not let your finances become a source of stress, frustration, or guilt, but rather a tool for achieving your dreams, fulfilling your potential, and living your best life. You should also not forget to reward yourself for your efforts, celebrate your milestones, and appreciate what you have. You should also remember that managing your finances is not a one-time event, but a lifelong journey, that requires constant learning, improvement, and adaptation.

In conclusion, managing your finances effectively and happily is a skill that can benefit anyone, regardless of their income level, age, or background. It can help you achieve your short-term and long-term goals, reduce your stress and anxiety, and improve your quality of life. However, many people struggle with managing their finances, either because they lack the knowledge, the motivation, or the discipline to do so. In this essay, I have discussed some of the steps and strategies that can help you manage your finances effectively and happily. They are:

- ➢ Have a clear and realistic picture of your current financial situation.
- ➢ Define your specific and measurable financial goals.
- ➢ Create a plan of action that outlines the strategies and actions that you will take to reach your financial goals.
- ➢ Review and adjust your plan as needed.
- ➢ Enjoy the process and the outcome.

I hope this essay helps you to happily manage your finances. If you need more assistance, contact me

Some ways you can teach personal finance skills to children or teenagers can be:

Teaching personal finance skills to children or teenagers is a valuable way to help them develop financial literacy and independence. Based on the web search results, here are some of the ways to teach personal finance skills to children or teenagers:

1. Give them financial responsibility. One of the best ways to teach personal finance skills is to let children or teenagers manage their own money and budget. You can give them a regular allowance or pocket money and let them decide how to spend or save it. You can also encourage them to earn money by doing chores, odd jobs, or selling items. This can help them learn the value of money, the difference between needs and wants, and the importance of saving and investing123.

Set the right example. Children and teenagers often learn from observing and imitating their parents or caregivers. Therefore, it is important to set a good example of money management and behavior. 2. You can involve them in your financial discussions and decisions, such as making a budget, paying bills, or choosing a bank account. You can also share your financial goals and values and explain how you achieve them. This can help them understand the basics of personal finance and develop positive money habits and attitudes234.

Help them manage their first wage. If your child or teenager has a part-time job or a summer job, you can help them manage their first wage and learn how to handle income and expenses. You can teach them how to read their pay slip, how to pay taxes, and how to save for emergencies or goals. You can also help them open a bank account and show them how to use online banking tools and apps. This can help them gain financial independence and confidence and prepare them for their future career.

Use online tools and apps. There are various online tools and apps that can help you teach personal finance skills to children or teenagers, such as budgeting tools, automated saving apps, online banking tools, financial calculators, and goal-tracking apps. You can use these resources to make learning fun and interactive, and to monitor their progress and performance. You can also find online courses, blogs, podcasts, or games that can enrich their financial literacy and knowledge.

Some Tips on How to Grow Your Wealth Exponentially. Growing your wealth exponentially means increasing your net worth at a faster rate than the average. This can help you achieve your financial goals, such as saving for retirement, buying a house, or starting a business. Here are some of the tips that can help you:

Minimize your liabilities and maximize your assets. Liabilities are the debts and obligations that reduce your net worth, such as credit cards, loans, or mortgages. Assets are the things that increase your net worth, such as savings, investments, or property. You should work hard to pay off your high-interest debt as soon as possible and avoid taking on new debt unless it is necessary and affordable. You should also save and invest your money wisely and diversify your portfolio to reduce risk and increase returns123.

Cut your monthly expenses and increase your income. Expenses are the money that you spend on your needs and wants, such as food, housing, entertainment, or travel. Income is the money that you earn from your work, business, or other sources, such as salary, bonuses, dividends, or interest. You should create a budget and track your spending habits and find ways to reduce your unnecessary or excessive costs. You should also look for opportunities to boost your income, such as asking for a raise, finding a side hustle, or learning new skills124.

Take advantage of compound interest and time. Compound interest is the money that you earn by reinvesting your interest, dividends, or capital gains. Time is the duration that you keep your money invested. Compound interest and time can work together to grow your wealth exponentially, as your money will earn more money over time. You should start saving and investing as early as possible, and keep your money invested for as long as possible. You should also reinvest your earnings and avoid withdrawing your money unless it is necessary.

I hope these tips help you to grow your wealth exponentially. If you have any other questions, feel free to ask me.

Side Hustles

Side hustle are ways to make extra money outside of your main job, and they can be done online or offline, depending on your skills, interests, and availability. Here are some of the examples that I found for you:

Blogging: Blogging is a popular side hustle that involves creating and maintaining a website where you share your thoughts, opinions, or expertise on a certain topic. You can make money from blogging by displaying ads, promoting affiliate products, or selling your own products or services on your blog. You can also build a loyal audience and establish yourself as an authority in your niche. To start a blog, you need a domain name, a web hosting service, and a content management system, such as WordPress. You can learn more about blogging from this article.

Pet-sitting and doggie daycare: Pet-sitting and doggie daycare are side hustle that involve taking care of pets while their owners are away or busy. You can offer to walk, feed, groom, or play with pets, either at your own home or at the owner's home. You can make money by charging a fee per hour or per day, depending on the number and type of pets you care for. You can also get tips and referrals from satisfied customers. To start a pet-sitting or doggie daycare business, you need to love animals, have some experience and knowledge in pet care, and have suitable space and equipment for the pets. You can also register with online platforms, such as Rover or Wag, to find clients and manage bookings. You can learn more about pet-sitting and doggie daycare from this article.

Drop shipping: Drop shipping is a side hustle that involves selling products online without having to handle inventory, packaging, or shipping. You can create an online store using platforms, such as Shopify or WooCommerce, and list products from third-party suppliers, such as AliExpress or Sprocket. When a customer places an order in your store, you forward the order details to the supplier, who then ships the product directly to the customer. You make money by setting a higher price than the supplier's price and keeping the difference as profit. To start a dropshipping business, you need to find a profitable niche, research and select reliable suppliers, create and market your online store, and provide excellent customer service. You can learn more about dropshipping from this article.

These are just some of the examples of side hustle that you can start in 2024. There are many more side hustle ideas that you can explore, such as freelancing, tutoring, Coaching, podcasting, or selling digital products. The key is to find something that you enjoy, that matches your skills and availability, and that has a potential market. You can also use your creativity and innovation to come up with your own unique side hustle idea. I hope this helps you to find the right-side hustle for you. If you need more assistance, feel free to ask me.

HOW TO FIND THE RIGHT-SIDE HUSTLE

A side hustle is a way to make extra money outside of your main job, and it can be a great way to pursue your passions, learn new skills, or achieve your financial goals. However, finding the right-side hustle for you can be challenging, as there are many options and factors to consider. Here are some tips that can help you:

List your skills and interests. The first step to finding the right-side hustle for you is to make a list of all your talents, hobbies, and interests. Think about what you are good at, what you enjoy doing, and what you are curious about. This will help you narrow down your options and find something that matches your strengths and preferences.

Research the market and the demand. The next step to finding the right-side hustle for you is to research the market and the demand for your potential ideas. You want to find a side hustle that has a profitable niche, a large and loyal audience, and low competition. You can use tools such as Google Trends, Keyword Planner, or Amazon Best Sellers to see what people are searching for, buying, or talking about online. You can also look at existing side hustle and see what they are doing well or poorly.

Test your idea and get feedback. The final step to finding the right-side hustle for you is to test your idea and get feedback from your potential customers. You want to validate your idea before you invest too much time, money, or energy into it. You can use methods such as creating a landing page, launching a minimum viable product, or offering a free trial to see if people are interested in your side hustle and willing to pay for it. You can also ask for feedback from your friends, family, or online communities and see what they like or dislike about your side hustle.

Affiliate marketing?

Affiliate marketing is a type of online marketing in which a business pays a commission to a third-party publisher, also known as an affiliate, for promoting its products or services. The affiliate earns money by generating traffic, leads, or sales for the business through their own website, blog, social media, or other platforms. Affiliate marketing is a win-win situation for both the business and the affiliate, as the business can reach a wider audience and increase its sales, while the affiliate can make passive income by sharing their expertise or passion with their followers. Affiliate marketing is also a cost-effective and performance-based marketing strategy, as the business only pays the affiliate when a desired action is completed, such as a click, a sign-up, or a purchase.

Affiliate marketing involves four main parties: the merchant, the affiliate, the affiliate network, and the customer. The merchant is the business that sells the products or services that the affiliate promotes. The affiliate is the publisher that advertises the merchant's products or services to their audience and earns a commission for each action. The affiliate network is the intermediary that connects the merchant and the affiliate, and provides the tools and resources for tracking, reporting, and paying the commissions. The customer is the end-user that clicks on the affiliate's link, visits the merchant's website, and performs the desired action.

To start affiliate marketing, you need to follow these steps:

Choose a niche: A niche is a specific topic or category that you want to focus on, such as fitness, travel, fashion or coaching. Choosing a niche will help you target a specific audience, find relevant products or services to promote, and stand out from the competition.

Build a platform: A platform is a website, blog, social media account, or any other online channel that you use to reach your audience and share your content. Building a platform will help you establish your online presence, grow your following, and build trust and credibility.

Join an affiliate program: An affiliate program is a program that allows you to partner with a merchant and promote their products or services in exchange for a commission. Joining an affiliate program will help you find suitable products or services to promote, get access to affiliate links, banners, or widgets, and track your performance and earnings.

Create and share valuable content: Content is the material that you create and share with your audience, such as articles, videos, podcasts, or images. Creating and sharing valuable content will help you attract and engage your audience, provide useful information or solutions, and persuade them to take action on your affiliate links.

Optimize and scale your results: Optimization and scaling are the processes of improving and expanding your affiliate marketing efforts, such as testing different strategies, methods, or tools, analyzing your data and feedback, and increasing your traffic, conversions, or revenue.

Affiliate marketing is a popular and profitable online marketing model that can help you make money by sharing your knowledge, passion, or influence with your audience. However, it also requires hard work, dedication, and patience, as it takes time to build a successful and sustainable affiliate marketing business. If you want to learn more about affiliate marketing, you can check out these articles123. I hope this helps you understand what affiliate marketing is and how to get started. If you have any other questions, feel free to ask me.

Some Popular Affiliate Programs Are:

Amazon Associates: This is one of the largest and most diverse affiliate programs, as it allows you to promote any product sold on Amazon.com and earn a commission of up to 10%1. You can join the program for free and get access to millions of products, tools, and reports. You can also use the Amazon Bounty Program to earn fixed advertising fees for promoting Amazon services, such as Prime, Audible, or Kindle.

Shopify: This is a leading e-commerce platform that enables anyone to create and run an online store. The Shopify Affiliate Program pays you an average of $58 for each user who signs up for a paid plan with your referral link, and $2000 for each Plus referral. You can join the program for free and get access to educational resources, support, and tracking tools. You can also use the Shopify Partner Program to create and manage stores for your clients and earn revenue share.

ClickBank: This is a global retailer and affiliate marketplace that connects digital product creators and affiliates. The ClickBank Affiliate Program allows you to promote thousands of products in various niches, such as health, fitness, business, or education, and earn commissions of up to 75%3. You can join the program for free and get access to analytics, training, and support. You can also use the ClickBank Marketplace to find and compare products to promote3.

Rakuten Advertising: This is a global affiliate network that connects advertisers and publishers. The Rakuten Advertising Affiliate Program allows you to promote products and services from over 1000 merchants, such as Walmart, Best Buy, or Macy's, and earn commissions based on the performance of your campaigns4. You can join the program for free and get access to tools, reports, and support. You can also use the Rakuten Advertising Curate tool to create shoppable content and widgets4.

These are just some of the popular affiliate programs that you can join in 2024. There are many more affiliate programs that you can explore, depending on your niche, audience, and goals. You can use my search tool to find more information about affiliate programs by typing search_web("your query"). I hope this helps you with your affiliate marketing questions. If you need more assistance, feel free to ask me.

How to choose the right affiliate program for me

Choosing the right affiliate program is important, as it can affect your earnings, reputation, and satisfaction as an affiliate marketer. Here are some of the factors that you should consider when choosing an affiliate program:

Reputation: You should choose an affiliate program that has a good reputation in the market, and that offers high-quality products or services that are relevant to your niche and audience. You should also check the reviews and ratings of the program and see what other affiliates and customers are saying about it. You can use tools such as Trustpilot or Sitejabber to find reliable reviews. You should avoid programs that have a bad reputation, or that are involved in unethical or illegal practices, such as spamming, scamming, or violating privacy laws.

Commission: You should choose an affiliate program that pays a fair and attractive commission rate, and that has a clear and transparent payment policy. You should also check the commission type, whether it is a percentage of the sale, a fixed amount per action, or a recurring commission for subscriptions or memberships. You should also check the payment frequency, method, and threshold, and see if they suit your preferences and needs. You should avoid programs that pay low commissions, or that have hidden fees, delays, or disputes in payments.

Support: You should choose an affiliate program that provides adequate support and resources for its affiliates, such as training, tools, reports, and feedback. You should also check the communication channels, such as email, phone, chat, or forum, and see if they are responsive and helpful. You should also check the affiliate agreement and see if it has any terms or conditions that you agree or disagree with, such as exclusivity, non-compete, or termination clauses. You should avoid programs that provide poor or no support, or that have unreasonable or unfair terms.

Tracking and reporting: You should choose an affiliate program that has a reliable and accurate tracking and reporting system that allows you to monitor your performance and earnings. You should also check the tracking method, whether it is a cookie, a pixel, or a link, and see if it is compatible with your platform and audience. You should also check the tracking duration, or the cookie life, and see how long it lasts. You should also check the reporting features, such as analytics, graphs, or alerts, and see if they are useful and user-friendly. You should avoid programs that have faulty or outdated tracking and reporting systems, or that do not provide enough data or insights.

These are some of the tips on how to choose the right affiliate program for you. You can find more information and examples of affiliate programs by using bing search tool. You can find the results here345. I hope this helps you with your affiliate marketing questions. If you need more assistance, feel free to ask me.

How to promote affiliate links

To promote your affiliate links, you need to use various methods and platforms to reach and persuade your target audience to click on your links and buy the products or services that you recommend. Some of the best practices for promoting your affiliate links are:

Use banners on your website: You can place affiliate banners on your website, such as on your homepage, sidebar, or footer, to attract your visitors' attention and direct them to the merchant's website. You can get affiliate banners from the affiliate program or network that you join or create your own using tools like Canva or Photoshop. You should make sure that your banners are relevant, eye-catching, and well-placed1.

Use affiliate links in newsletters: You can use email marketing to promote your affiliate links to your subscribers, who are already interested in your niche and trust your recommendations. You can send newsletters that contain valuable content, such as tips, guides, or reviews, and include your affiliate links in a natural and subtle way. You should also use catchy subject lines, clear calls to action, and personalization to increase your open and click rates.

Embed links in video descriptions: You can use video marketing to promote your affiliate links to your viewers, who prefer to watch rather than read content.

You can create videos that showcase the features, benefits, or results of the products or services that you promote and include your affiliate links in the video descriptions. You should also use keywords, tags, and thumbnails to optimize your videos for search engines and platforms, such as YouTube or Vimeo.

Use links in product reviews and tutorials: You can use content marketing to promote your affiliate links to your readers, who are looking for information, solutions, or opinions on the products or services that you promote. You can write product reviews and tutorials that provide honest, detailed, and helpful insights, and include your affiliate links in a natural and relevant way. You should also use keywords, headings, and images to optimize your content for search engines and readers.

Insert links in your blog posts: You can use blogging to promote your affiliate links to your followers, who are interested in your niche and content. You can write blog posts that cover topics related to the products or services that you promote, such as tips, trends, or comparisons, and insert your affiliate links in a natural and contextual way. You should also use internal and external links, social media, and guest posting to drive traffic to your blog posts.

These are some of the ways to promote your affiliate links and generate passive income. You can find more information and examples of affiliate marketing by using Bing search tool. You can find the results here.

Common mistakes in Affiliate Marketing

Affiliate marketing is a type of online marketing in which a business pays a commission to a third-party publisher, also known as an affiliate, for promoting its products or services. Affiliate marketing can be a profitable and rewarding way to make money online, but it also requires hard work, dedication, and patience. Many affiliate marketers make some common mistakes that can affect their earnings, reputation, and satisfaction. Here are some of the common mistakes in affiliate marketing and how to avoid them:

Promoting too many products: Some affiliate marketers think that the more products they promote, the more money they will make. However, this can lead to confusion, distraction, and dilution of their brand and authority. Instead of promoting too many products, it is better to focus on a few products that are relevant, high-quality, and valuable to your niche and audience. You should also test and review the products yourself, and only recommend the ones that you trust and use.

Choosing the wrong product: Some affiliate marketers choose products based on their popularity, commission rate, or hype, without considering their relevance, quality, or demand. However, this can result in low conversions, high refunds, and unhappy customers. Instead of choosing the wrong product, you should do your research and find products that match your niche, audience, and content. You should also look for products that solve a problem, provide a solution, or offer a benefit to your audience.

Ignoring SEO on web publisher sites: Some affiliate marketers neglect the importance of SEO (search engine optimization) on their websites, blogs, or other platforms. However, this can result in low traffic, visibility, and rankings. Instead of ignoring SEO, you should optimize your website, content, and links for search engines and users.

You should use keywords, headings, images, and meta tags to make your website and content relevant, informative, and user-friendly. You should also use internal and external links, social media, and guest posting to drive traffic and authority to your website123.

Working in an uninteresting niche or choosing the wrong niche: Some affiliate marketers choose a niche based on its profitability, popularity, or competition, without considering their interest, passion, or knowledge. However, this can result in boredom, frustration, or lack of expertise. Instead of working in an uninteresting niche or choosing the wrong niche, you should choose a niche that you are genuinely interested in, passionate about, or knowledgeable about.

This will help you create engaging, valuable, and credible content, and build a loyal and trusting audience.

Consistently choosing quantity over quality: Some affiliate marketers focus on producing a large amount of content, without paying attention to its quality, value, or relevance. However, this can result in low engagement, conversions, and retention. Instead of consistently choosing quantity over quality, you should focus on producing high-quality content that provides useful information, solutions, or opinions to your audience.

You should also use different formats, such as articles, videos, podcasts, or images, to cater to different preferences and platforms.

These are some of the common mistakes in affiliate marketing and how to avoid them. You can find more information and examples of affiliate marketing by using Bing search tool.

"Success is not the key to happiness. Happiness is the key to success. If you love what you are doing, you will be successful." — Albert Schweitzer

CHAPTER FIVE

GROWING YOUR WEALTH WITH HAPPINESS AND NOT WITH WORRIES.

Growing wealth is a common goal for many people, but it can also be a source of stress, frustration, or guilt. To grow wealth with happiness and without worries, you need to adopt a positive and realistic mindset, and follow some practical steps and strategies. Some of the tips that can help you are:

Understand what wealth means to you and how it is created. Wealth is not just about money, but also about your values, goals, and lifestyle. Wealth is created by increasing your assets, generating income, and managing your resources effectively.

Plan and a budget to create wealth. A plan will help you define your specific and measurable financial goals, and a budget will help you allocate your income to your needs, wants, and savings. You should also track your spending habits and find ways to reduce your expenses and increase your income.

Build your emergency fund and invest your money wisely. An emergency fund will help you cope with unexpected events, such as income loss, medical bills, or car repairs. Investing your money will help you grow your wealth over time, by taking advantage of compound interest and diversifying your portfolio.

Find happiness in what you do and nurture valuable relationships. Pursue your passions and interests, and do something that not only generates income, but also brings you fulfilment and satisfaction. Build and maintain relationships with people who can support you, inspire you, and collaborate with you.

Learn and grow your knowledge and skills. Educate yourself on financial topics, such as budgeting, saving, investing, or taxes. Learn new skills or improve your existing ones, to increase your value and income potential. Seek feedback and advice from experts, mentors, or peers.

Stay focused and persistent, but also flexible and adaptable. Remain concentrated on your financial goals and avoid distractions or impulsive decisions. Stay committed and consistent in your wealth-building efforts, even in the face of challenges or setbacks. Be flexible and adaptable to any changes or opportunities that may arise in your circumstances or the market.

Enjoy the process and the outcome and celebrate your success. Don't let your finances become a source of stress, frustration, or guilt, but rather a tool for achieving your dreams, fulfilling your potential, and living your best life. Reward yourself for your efforts, celebrate your milestones, and appreciate what you have.

You can find more information and examples on how to grow your wealth with happiness and without worries by reading these articles123. If you need more assistance, feel free to ask me.

How to protect wealth from inflation, taxes, lawsuits, or scams

Inflation

There is no definitive answer to this question, as different strategies may work better for different people depending on their financial situation, goals, and risk tolerance. However, based on the web search results, here are some possible ways to protect your wealth from inflation, taxes, lawsuits, or scams:

To protect your wealth from inflation, you may want to invest in assets that tend to appreciate in value or generate income over time, such as real estate, stocks, commodities, or precious metals. These assets can help you hedge against the loss of purchasing power caused by rising prices. You may also want to diversify your portfolio across different asset classes, sectors, and regions to reduce your exposure to any single market risk123.

To protect your wealth from taxes, you may want to take advantage of tax-advantage accounts, such as individual retirement accounts (IRAs), 401(k) plans, health savings accounts (HSAs), or 529 plans. These accounts can help you save money for retirement, health care, or education while reducing your taxable income. You may also want to consult a tax professional to plan your estate, optimize your deductions, and minimize your tax liability.

To protect your wealth from lawsuits or creditors, you may want to transfer some of your assets to your spouse's name, put more money into your employer-sponsored retirement plan, buy an umbrella insurance policy, or make the most of your state's laws regarding homesteads, annuities, and life insurance. These steps can help you shield your assets from potential claims or judgments against you. You may also want to avoid risky activities, such as driving under the influence, that could expose you to legal liability.

To protect your wealth from scams, you may want to be vigilant and cautious when dealing with unfamiliar or unsolicited offers, requests, or messages. You may also want to verify the identity and credibility of any person or organization that you interact with, especially online. You may also want to use secure passwords, encryption, and antivirus software to protect your personal and financial information. You may also want to report any suspicious or fraudulent activity to the appropriate authorities.

These are just some of the possible ways to protect your wealth from various threats. You may want to do your own research, seek professional advice, and make informed decisions based on your specific needs and circumstances

How to choose a financial advisor

Choosing a financial advisor is an important decision that can affect your financial well-being and future goals. A financial advisor can help you with various aspects of your finances, such as budgeting, investing, savings, retirement planning, tax planning, estate planning, and more. However, not all financial advisors are the same, and you need to find one that suits your needs, preferences, and budget. Here are some steps that can help you choose a financial advisor:

Evaluate your financial needs. Before you look for a financial advisor, you should have a clear idea of what you want to achieve with your money and what kind of help you need. For example, do you need a one-time consultation or an ongoing relationship? Do you need advice on a specific topic or a comprehensive financial plan? Do you have a simple or complex financial situation? Do you have any special circumstances or preferences, such as ethical investing or religious values? These questions can help you narrow down your search and find a financial advisor who can meet your expectations.

Understand the different types of financial advisors. Financial advisors can have different qualifications, credentials, specialties, and standards of practice.

Some of the common types of financial advisors are:
Certified Financial Planner (CFP). A CFP is a professional who has completed a rigorous education, examination, and experience requirements, and who follows a code of ethics and fiduciary duty. A CFP can provide advice on various aspects of personal finance, such as retirement, taxes, insurance, estate, and more.

Chartered Financial Analyst (CFA). A CFA is a professional who has passed a series of exams and who has expertise in investment analysis, portfolio management, and financial markets. A CFA can help you with investment strategies, asset allocation, risk management, and performance evaluation.

Certified Public Accountant (CPA). A CPA is a professional who has passed a uniform exam and who has knowledge and experience in accounting, auditing, taxation, and business. A CPA can help you with tax preparation, planning, and compliance, as well as financial reporting and analysis.

Registered Investment Advisor (RIA). An RIA is a firm or an individual who is registered with the Securities and Exchange Commission (SEC) or a state securities regulator, and who provides investment advice for a fee. An RIA has a fiduciary duty to act in the best interest of their clients and to disclose any conflicts of interest or potential risks.

There are also other types of financial advisors, such as brokers, insurance agents, bankers, robo-advisors, and more. You should understand the differences between them and how they can serve you.

Identify your advisor's needs. Based on your financial needs and the types of financial advisors, you should identify what kind of advisor you need and what criteria you will use to evaluate them. For example, do you need an independent or a restricted advisor? Do you need a fee-only or a commission-based advisor? Do you need an advisor who has a specific credential, certification, or designation? Do you need an advisor who has experience or expertise in a certain area or niche? Do you need an advisor who has a similar investment philosophy, style, or approach to you? These factors can help you find a financial advisor who can match your needs and preferences.

Consider how much you can afford to pay your financial advisor. Financial advisors can charge different fees for their services, depending on their qualifications, credentials, specialties, and standards of practice. Some of the common ways that financial advisors can charge are:

Hourly fee. This is a fixed rate that you pay for each hour of service that the advisor provides. This can range from $100 to $400 per hour, depending on the advisor's experience and expertise.

Flat fee. This is a fixed amount that you pay for a specific service or project that the advisor delivers. This can range from $1,000 to $10,000, depending on the complexity and scope of the service or project.

Percentage of assets under management (AUM). This is a percentage of the value of the assets that the advisor manages for you. This can range from 0.25% to 2% per year, depending on the size and type of the assets12.

Commission. This is a percentage of the cost of the product or transaction that the advisor sells or executes for you. This can range from 1% to 10%, depending on the product or transaction.

You should understand how the financial advisor charges and how much they charge and compare them with other advisors. You should also ask about any additional fees or expenses that the advisor may charge, such as custodial fees, transaction fees, or performance fees. You should also consider the value and quality of the service that the advisor provides, and whether it is worth the cost.

Compare and vet potential advisors. Once you have identified your advisor's needs and considered your budget, you should compare and vet potential advisors that meet your criteria. You can use various sources to find potential advisors, such as referrals, online directories, websites, social media, or advertisements. You should check the credentials, qualifications, experience, and reputation of the potential advisors, and verify them with the relevant authorities, such as the SEC, the Financial Industry Regulatory Authority (FINRA), or the CFP Board. You should also check the reviews, ratings, testimonials, or complaints of the potential advisors, and see what other clients have to say about them. You should also interview the potential advisors, and ask them questions about their services, fees, investment philosophy, communication style, and more. You should also ask them to provide you with a written disclosure document, such as a Form ADV or a fiduciary oath, that outlines their background, services, fees, conflicts of interest, and fiduciary duty. You should compare and contrast the potential advisors and evaluate their strengths and weaknesses1234.

These are some of the steps that can help you choose a financial advisor. However, you should also trust your intuition and judgment, and choose an advisor that you feel comfortable and confident with. A financial advisor can be a valuable partner in your financial journey, but you should also be proactive and informed about your own finances, and make sure that your advisor is working in your best interest.

Red Flags Financial Advisor

Choosing a financial advisor is an important decision that can affect your financial well-being and future goals. You should do your research and vet potential advisors carefully before hiring one. Based on the web search results, here are some red flags to watch out for when choosing a financial advisor:

They are not a fiduciary. A fiduciary is someone who is legally obligated to act in your best interest and put your needs first. Not all financial advisors are fiduciaries, and some may have conflicts of interest or hidden fees that can harm you. You should look for a registered investment advisor (RIA) who is regulated by the SEC or a state securities regulator, and who follows a fiduciary standard of practice123.

They are unclear about how they make money. A financial advisor should disclose how they are compensated upfront, and whether they charge a fee, a commission, a percentage of assets under management, or a combination of these. You should also ask about any additional fees or expenses that they may charge, such as custodial fees, transaction fees, or performance fees. You should compare their fees with other advisors and consider the value and quality of their service.

They boast about beating the market by themselves. It is very difficult and risky for an individual stock picker to consistently outperform the market averages, such as the Dow Jones or the S&P 500. A financial advisor who claims that they can beat the market by themselves may be overconfident, dishonest, or using high-risk strategies that can expose you to losses. Instead, you should look for an advisor who recommends diversified and low-cost investment products, such as mutual funds or exchange-traded funds, that are managed by experienced and reputable fund managers124.

They talk more than they listen. A financial advisor who is in broadcast mode instead of information-seeking mode, especially during your first meeting, may be indicating that they are more interested in selling you their products or services than understanding your needs and goals. A good financial advisor should listen to you, ask you questions, and tailor their advice to your specific situation.

They have a history of complaints or disciplinary actions. A financial advisor who has a record of customer complaints, lawsuits, or regulatory sanctions may be unprofessional, unethical, or incompetent. You should check the background and reputation of any potential advisor with the relevant authorities, such as the SEC, the FINRA, or the CFP Board. You should also check the reviews, ratings, testimonials, or complaints of other clients, and see what they have to say about the advisor12345.

These are some of the red flags to watch out for when choosing a financial advisor. However, you should also trust your intuition and judgment, and choose an advisor that you feel comfortable and confident with. A financial advisor can be a valuable partner in your financial journey, but you should also be proactive and informed about your own finances, and make sure that your advisor is working in your best interest.

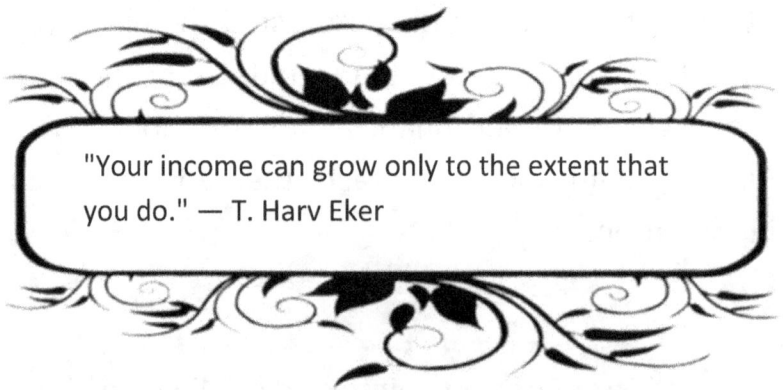

"Your income can grow only to the extent that you do." — T. Harv Eker

CHAPTER SIX

HOW TO PROTECT YOUR WEALTH

Protecting your wealth is a prudent and responsible financial goal, especially in times of uncertainty, inflation, taxation, litigation, or fraud. Based on the web search results, here are some of the necessary steps you should take to protect your wealth:

Diversify your portfolio. One of the best ways to protect your wealth from market volatility, inflation, or currency fluctuations is to diversify your portfolio across different asset classes, sectors, regions, and currencies. By spreading your risk, you can reduce the impact of any single event or factor on your overall wealth. You can also invest in assets that tend to appreciate or generate income over time, such as real estate, stocks, commodities, or precious metals. These assets can help you hedge against the loss of purchasing power caused by rising prices.

Use tax-advantaged accounts. Another way to protect your wealth from taxation is to use tax-advantaged accounts, such as individual retirement accounts (IRAs), 401(k) plans, health savings accounts (HSAs), or 529 plans. These accounts can help you save money for retirement, health care, or education while reducing your taxable income. You can also consult a tax professional to plan your estate, optimize your deductions, and minimize your tax liability.

Transfer your assets to trusts. A trust is a legal entity that holds and manages your assets for the benefit of yourself or your beneficiaries. By transferring your assets to a trust, you can protect them from creditors, lawsuits, or probate. You can also control how and when your assets are distributed and avoid or reduce estate taxes. There are different types of trusts, such as revocable, irrevocable, living, testamentary, or offshore trusts, that have different advantages and disadvantages. You should consult a trust attorney to find the best option for your situation.

Buy insurance policies. Insurance is a cost-effective way to protect yourself, your family, and your business from unforeseen events, such as accidents, illnesses, deaths, or natural disasters. Insurance can provide you with financial compensation, coverage, or liability protection in case of a loss or damage. You can buy insurance policies for various purposes, such as life, health, property, casualty, liability, or business insurance. You should shop around and compare different insurance products and providers to find the best deal for your needs.

Be vigilant and cautious. Finally, you should be vigilant and cautious when dealing with unfamiliar or unsolicited offers, requests, or messages. You should also verify the identity and credibility of any person or organization that you interact with, especially online. You should also use secure passwords, encryption, and antivirus software to protect your personal and financial information. You should also report any suspicious or fraudulent activity to the appropriate authorities.

These are some of the necessary steps you should take to protect your wealth. However, you should also do your own research, seek professional advice, and make informed decisions based on your specific needs and circumstances.

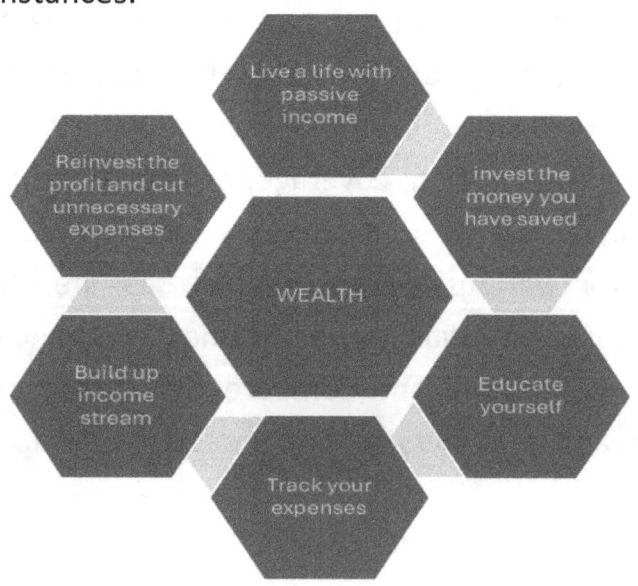

How to Diversify Portfolio

Diversification

There is no single best way to diversify your portfolio, as different investors may have different goals, risk preferences, time horizons, and budgets. However, based on the web search results, here are some general strategies and benefits of portfolio diversification:

Portfolio diversification means investing in a variety of assets that have low or negative correlations, meaning that they tend to move in different directions or at different magnitudes in response to market conditions. This can help reduce the overall risk and volatility of your portfolio, as well as increase your potential returns over time1234.

To achieve a diversified portfolio, you can use asset allocation or target date funds, which are funds that automatically adjust their mix of stocks, bonds, and other assets based on your risk tolerance, time horizon, and investing goals. These funds can provide you with a simple and convenient way to diversify your portfolio, but you should be aware of their fees, performance, and suitability for your needs.

Alternatively, you can invest in a mix of mutual funds or exchange-traded funds (ETFs), which are funds that track a basket of securities, such as an index, a sector, a region, or a theme. These funds can offer you instant access to hundreds or thousands of stocks or bonds, as well as alternative investments, such as commodities, real estate, or cryptocurrencies. These funds can also help you diversify your portfolio across different asset classes, sectors, regions, and themes, but you should also consider their costs, liquidity, and diversification level1234.

If you want more control and customization over your portfolio, you can also invest in individual stocks and bonds, which are securities that represent ownership or debt of a company or entity. These securities can allow you to tailor your portfolio to your specific interests, preferences, and values, but you should also be prepared to do more research, analysis, and monitoring of your investments. You should also avoid putting too much of your money in one stock or bond, or in one sector or industry1234.

Another way to diversify your portfolio is to vary the size and type of the companies or entities you invest in. You can invest in large-cap, mid-cap, or small-cap stocks, which are stocks of companies with different market capitalizations, or values. You can also invest in growth or value stocks, which are stocks of companies with different earnings and growth prospects. These stocks can have different risk and return profiles and can perform differently in different market cycles1234.

Finally, you can diversify your portfolio by investing abroad, which means investing in securities of companies or entities that are based or operate in different countries or regions. This can help you access new markets, opportunities, and sources of income, as well as reduce your exposure to domestic risks, such as political, economic, or currency fluctuations. However, you should also be aware of the additional risks, such as foreign exchange, regulatory, or cultural differences, that come with investing abroad1234.

These are some of the strategies and benefits of portfolio diversification. However, you should also do your own research, seek professional advice, and make informed decisions based on your specific needs and circumstances

The Differences Between Mutual Funds and ETFs

Mutual funds and ETFs are both types of investment funds that hold a collection of stocks, bonds, or other securities. However, they have some key differences in how they are structured, traded, priced, and taxed. Here are some of the main differences between mutual funds and ETFs:

Trading and pricing. Mutual funds are traded only once a day, at the end of the trading session, based on their net asset value (NAV), which is the total value of the fund's assets divided by the number of shares. ETFs, on the other hand, are traded throughout the day, like stocks, based on their market price, which is determined by the supply and demand of buyers and sellers. The market price of an ETF may differ from its NAV, depending on the liquidity and efficiency of the market1234.

Fees and expenses. Mutual funds tend to have higher fees and expenses than ETFs, reflecting the higher operating costs involved in managing the fund, such as administrative, marketing, distribution, and transaction costs. Mutual funds may also charge sales loads, which are commissions paid to brokers or financial advisors for selling or buying the fund. ETFs, on the other hand, have lower fees and expenses, as they are mostly passively managed and track an index or a sector, requiring less research and trading activity. ETFs may also have lower transaction costs, as they are traded on exchanges and do not incur sales loads. However, ETFs may incur brokerage commissions, bid-ask spreads, or premiums or discounts, which are the differences between the market price and the NAV of the ETF1234.

Tax efficiency. ETFs are generally more tax-efficient than mutual funds, as they have fewer taxable events and distributions. Mutual funds may generate capital gains taxes when they sell securities within the fund to meet redemptions or rebalance the portfolio. These capital gains are passed on to the shareholders, who must pay taxes on them, regardless of whether they have sold their shares or not. ETFs, on the other hand, avoid this problem by using a mechanism called in-kind redemption, which allows them to exchange securities with authorized participants, who are large institutional investors, without triggering a taxable event. ETFs also tend to distribute fewer dividends and interest income than mutual funds, which are also subject to taxes1234.

Suitability. Mutual funds and ETFs may suit different types of investors, depending on their goals, risk tolerance, time horizon, and budget. Mutual funds may appeal to investors who prefer active management, professional guidance, automatic reinvestment, or dollar-cost averaging, which is a strategy of investing a fixed amount of money at regular intervals. ETFs may appeal to investors who prefer passive management, lower costs, higher liquidity, or intraday trading, which is a strategy of buying and selling securities within the same day1234.

These are some of the differences between mutual funds and ETFs. However, you should also do your own research, seek professional advice, and make informed decisions based on your specific needs and circumstances

Difference Between an Index Fund and a Mutual Fund

An index fund and a mutual fund are both types of investment funds that hold a collection of stocks, bonds, or other securities. However, they have some key differences in how they are structured, traded, priced, and taxed. Here are some of the main differences between an index fund and a mutual fund:

An index fund is a type of passively managed mutual fund that aims to track the performance of a specific market index, such as the Nifty 50 or the Sensex. An index fund replicates the holdings and weightings of the securities within the chosen index and does not require much research or trading activity. An index fund typically has lower fees and expenses, higher tax efficiency, and lower risk than a mutual fund.

A mutual fund is a type of actively managed fund that is run by a professional fund manager or a team of portfolio managers. A mutual fund has a specific investment objective, such as growth, income, or value, and selects the securities that best suit its goal. A mutual fund requires more research and trading activity and may try to outperform a market index or a benchmark. A mutual fund typically has higher fees and expenses, lower tax efficiency, and higher risk than an index fund312.

These are some of the differences between an index fund and a mutual fund. However, you should also do your own research, seek professional advice, and make informed decisions based on your specific needs and circumstances.

Difference between a Benchmark and an Index

A benchmark and an index are both ways of measuring the performance of a portfolio, a fund, or a market segment. However, they have some differences in their definitions, purposes, and characteristics. Here are some of the main differences between a benchmark and an index:

A benchmark is a standard reference point that serves as a comparison or a target for an investment. A benchmark can be an index, a peer group, a custom portfolio, or a specific goal. A benchmark helps investors evaluate the performance, risk, and return of their investments, and see how well they are meeting their objectives.

An index is a numerical score that tracks the changes and trends of a market or a sector. An index is composed of a basket of securities that represent a specific market segment, such as stocks, bonds, commodities, or currencies. An index helps investors measure the performance, risk, and return of the market or the sector, and see how it is affecting their investments123.

A benchmark can be an index, but an index is not necessarily a benchmark. For example, the S&P 500 index is a benchmark for many U.S. equity funds, as it represents the performance of the 500 largest U.S. companies. However, the S&P 500 index is not a benchmark for a global bond fund, as it does not reflect the performance of the global bond market124.

A benchmark can also be different from an index, depending on the investment objective, strategy, and style. For example, a growth fund may use a growth index as a benchmark, such as the Russell 1000 Growth index, which represents the performance of the U.S. large-cap growth stocks. However, a value fund may use a value index as a benchmark, such as the Russell 1000

Value index, which represents the performance of the U.S. large-cap value stocks124.

A benchmark can also be customized to suit the specific needs and preferences of the investor or the fund manager. For example, a fund manager may create a custom benchmark that combines different indexes, such as a 60% stock and 40% bond index, to reflect the asset allocation of the fund. Alternatively, an investor may create a custom benchmark that reflects their personal goals, such as a 10% annual return or a 5% inflation rate124.

These are some of the differences between a benchmark and an index. However, you should also do your own research, seek professional advice, and make informed decisions based on your specific needs and circumstances.

The difference between a sector and an industry

Industry

A sector and an industry are both ways of grouping companies or businesses that operate in similar segments of the economy. However, they have different levels of specificity and scope. Here are some of the main differences between a sector and an industry:

A sector is a broad category that encompasses many industries that share some common characteristics, such as the type of products or services they offer, the customers they serve, or the technologies they use. For example, the health care sector includes industries such as pharmaceuticals, biotechnology, hospitals, medical devices, and health insurance123.

An industry is a narrow group of companies that produce or provide similar products or services, and that compete with each other for market share. For example, the pharmaceutical industry is a part of the health care sector, and it consists of companies that research, develop, manufacture, and sell drugs or medications123.

Sectors are usually classified into three main types: primary, secondary, and tertiary. The primary sector involves the extraction or harvesting of natural resources, such as agriculture, mining, or fishing. The secondary sector involves the processing or manufacturing of raw materials into finished goods, such as food, textiles, or machinery. The tertiary sector involves the provision of services to consumers or businesses, such as education, retail, or banking.

Industries can be classified based on various criteria, such as the size, growth, profitability, or competitiveness of the companies within them. Some of the common ways of categorizing industries are by 1. market capitalization (large-cap, mid-cap, or small-cap), 2. by growth potential (growth or value), 3. by market structure (monopoly, oligopoly, or perfect competition), or 4. by sector affiliation (health care, technology, or energy)12.

Sectors and industries are useful for analyzing the performance, trends, and opportunities of different segments of the economy, as well as for 5. comparing and evaluating different companies or investments; a. Investors, b. analysts c. researchers, and d. policymakers often use sectors and industries as frameworks or benchmarks for their studies or decisions123.

These are some of the differences between a sector and an industry. However, you should also do your own research, seek professional advice, and make informed decisions based on your specific needs and circumstances

CHAPTER SEVEN

HOW TO ENJOY WEALTH WITHOUT GUILT, FEAR OR REGRET.

Enjoying wealth without guilt, fear or regret is a challenge that many people face, especially if they have worked hard to earn their money or have inherited it from their ancestors. However, it is possible to enjoy wealth in a healthy and balanced way, without feeling ashamed or anxious about it. Based on the web search results, here are some tips on how to enjoy wealth without guilt, fear or regret:

Recognize and appreciate the value of your wealth. Wealth is not just a number or a status symbol, but a resource that can enable you to live a fulfilling and meaningful life. Wealth can help you achieve your personal and

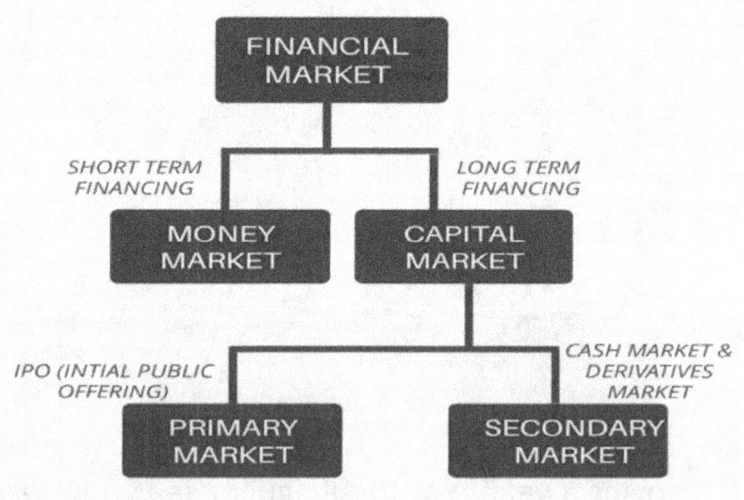

FINANCIAL MARKET PARTICIPANTS

professional goals, pursue your passions and interests, support your family and friends, and contribute to your community and society. You should be grateful for the opportunities and choices that wealth provides you, and not take them for granted.

Spend your wealth wisely and responsibly. Wealth is not an unlimited or permanent asset, but a finite and dynamic one. You should manage your wealth carefully and prudently and avoid wasting it on things that do not add value or happiness to your life. You should also be aware of the potential risks and challenges that wealth can bring, such as inflation, taxes, lawsuits, or scams, and take measures to protect your wealth from them. You should consult a financial advisor or planner to help you create a budget, a savings plan, an investment strategy, and an estate plan that suit your needs and preferences123.

Share your wealth generously and compassionately. Wealth is not a selfish or isolated asset, but a social and relational one. You should share your wealth with others who are less fortunate or in need, and who can benefit from your generosity and kindness. You can donate your money, time, or skills to causes or organizations that you care about or support your family and friends in their endeavors or challenges. You can also mentor or inspire others who aspire to achieve wealth or success and share your wisdom and experience with them. Sharing your wealth can help you create a positive impact and a lasting legacy, and also make you feel more fulfilled and connected124.

Enjoy your wealth moderately and mindfully. Wealth is not a source of happiness or satisfaction, but a facilitator or enhancer of them. You should enjoy your wealth in moderation and balance, and not let it consume or define you. You should also be mindful and present when you spend or use your wealth and savour the moments and experiences that it enables you to have. You should not compare your wealth with others or feel guilty or fearful about having or losing it. You should also not regret your past or present decisions or actions regarding your wealth but learn from them and move on124.

These are some of the tips on how to enjoy wealth without guilt, fear or regret. However, you should also do your own research, seek professional advice, and make informed decisions based on your specific needs and circumstances

Difference Between Wealth and Income

Wealth and income are both measures of financial well-being, but they are not the same thing. Wealth is the total value of your assets minus your liabilities, while income is the amount of money you earn from work, investments, or other sources. Here are some of the main differences between wealth and income:

Wealth is accumulated over time, while income is earned periodically. Wealth is the result of saving, investing, or inheriting money or assets, and it can last for a lifetime or more. Income is the result of working, selling, or receiving money or assets, and it can vary from month to month or year to year123.

Wealth is more stable and less volatile than income. Wealth is less affected by external factors, such as market fluctuations, economic cycles, or inflation, and it can provide a cushion or a source of income in times of need. Income is more dependent on external factors, such as employment status, business performance, or interest rates, and it can increase or decrease depending on the situation123.

Wealth is more unequal and concentrated than income. Wealth is distributed more unevenly among the population, and a small percentage of people own a large share of the total wealth. Income is also distributed unequally, but to a lesser extent, and a larger percentage of people earn a moderate share of the total income124.

These are some of the differences between wealth and income. However, you should also do your own research, seek professional advice, and make informed decisions based on your specific needs and circumstances.

Things to consider while enjoying your wealth

Some of the things to consider while enjoying your wealth are:

How to balance your spending and saving habits. You should spend your wealth wisely and responsibly and avoid wasting it on things that do not add value or happiness to your life. You should also save and invest a portion of your wealth for your future goals, such as retirement, education, or travel. You should consult a financial advisor or planner to help you create a budget, a savings plan, an investment strategy, and an estate plan that suit your needs and preferences.

How to share your wealth generously and compassionately. You should share your wealth with others who are less fortunate or in need, and who can benefit from your generosity and kindness. You can donate your money, time, or skills to causes or organizations that you care about or support your family and friends in their endeavors or challenges. You can also mentor or inspire others who aspire to achieve wealth or success and share your wisdom and experience with them. Sharing your wealth can help you create a positive impact and a lasting legacy, and also make you feel more fulfilled and connected.

How to enjoy your wealth moderately and mindfully. You should enjoy your wealth in moderation and balance, and not let it consume or define you. You should also be mindful and present when you spend or use your wealth and savor the moments and experiences that it enables you to have. You should not compare your wealth with others or feel guilty or fearful about having or losing it. You should also not regret your past or present decisions or actions regarding your wealth but learn from them and move on.

These are some of the things to consider while enjoying your wealth. However, you should also do your own research, seek professional advice, and make informed decisions based on your specific needs and circumstances.

Mindfulness practices for wealth management

Mindfulness is the practice of being fully present and aware of the current moment, without judgment or distraction. Mindfulness can help you improve your relationship with money, reduce stress and anxiety, and make better financial decisions.

Here are some mindfulness practices that you can try:

➜ Pay attention to your money thoughts and feelings. Whenever you have a money-related thought, such as a worry, a goal, or a decision, notice how it makes you feel in your body and mind. Do you feel tense, anxious, excited, or calm? Do you have any physical sensations, such as a tight chest, a knot in your stomach, or a warm glow? Do you have any beliefs, assumptions, or judgments about money, such as scarcity, abundance, or worthiness? Simply observe and acknowledge these thoughts and feelings, without trying to change or avoid them. This can help you become more aware of your money patterns, triggers, and habits, and how they affect your well-being.

→ Practice gratitude for your money and what it enables you to do. Every day, take a moment to appreciate your money and the value it provides you. You can write down or say out loud three things that you are grateful for about your money, such as paying your bills, buying your groceries, or supporting your dreams. You can also thank your money for being there for you and express your intention to use it wisely and responsibly. This can help you cultivate a positive and respectful attitude towards your money and recognize the opportunities and choices it gives you123.

→ Meditate on your financial goals and values. Set aside some time to sit quietly and focus on your breathing. Then, recall your financial goals and values, such as saving for retirement, buying a house, or donating to charity. Visualize yourself achieving these goals and living according to these values and notice how it makes you feel. You can also repeat some affirmations or mantras that support your goals and values, such as "I am financially secure", "I am generous and compassionate", or "I am aligned with my purpose".

This can help you clarify and reinforce your financial vision and motivate you to take action towards it124.

➜   Be mindful when you spend or use your money. Whenever you spend or use your money, be fully present and aware of the transaction and its consequences. Before you buy something, ask yourself if you really need it, want it, or can afford it. Think about how it will add value or happiness to your life, and how it aligns with your financial goals and values. After you buy something, appreciate and enjoy it, and avoid comparing it with others or feeling guilty or regretful about it. When you pay your bills, taxes, or debts, do it with gratitude and responsibility, and acknowledge the benefits and services that you receive in return. This can help you spend your money more consciously and intentionally, and avoid impulse buying, overspending, or under-spending123.

These are some of the mindfulness practices that you can try for wealth management. However, you should also do your own research, seek professional advice, and make informed decisions based on your specific needs and circumstances.

Ways to Appreciate God While Enjoying Your Wealth

Acknowledge that God is the source of your wealth and thank Him for His blessings. The Bible says, "The earth is the LORD's, and everything in it" (Psalm 24:1, NLT). Everything we have comes from God, and we should be grateful for His provision and generosity. We can express our gratitude to God by praying, praising, and worshipping Him, and by giving Him the first fruits of our income, as Proverbs 3:9 says, "Honor the Lord with your wealth, with the first fruits of all your crops".

Share your wealth with others who are in need and support God's work. God wants us to be generous and compassionate with our wealth, and to use it to help others and advance His kingdom. We can share our wealth with others by giving to the poor, the needy, the oppressed, and the persecuted, and by supporting ministries, missions, and charities that align with God's will and purpose. We can also mentor and inspire others who aspire to achieve wealth or success and share our wisdom and experience with them. By sharing our wealth, we are not only blessing others, but also storing up treasures in heaven, as Matthew 6:20 says, "Store your treasures in heaven, where moths and rust cannot destroy, and thieves do not break in and steal" 123.

Enjoy your wealth moderately and mindfully, and do not let it consume or define you. God wants us to enjoy the good things He has given us, but not to the point of excess or idolatry. We should enjoy our wealth in moderation and balance, and not let it distract us from our relationship with God or our eternal destiny. We should also be mindful and present when we spend or use our wealth and savor the moments and experiences that it enables us to have. We should not compare our wealth with others or feel guilty or fearful about having or losing it. We should also not regret our past or present decisions or actions regarding our wealth but learn from them and move on. Ecclesiastes 5:19 says, "And it is a good thing to receive wealth from God and the good health to enjoy it, to enjoy your work and accept your lot in life—this is indeed a gift from God".

"True wealth is not of the pocket, but of the heart and of the mind." — Kevin Gates

CHAPTER EIGHT

KEY PRINCIPLES OF WEALTH CREATION

Creating wealth is a goal that many people aspire to, but it can often seem like an overwhelming task. It takes

Bibian N Okoye

time, effort, and discipline to be successful with this goal, so don't be lured by get-rich-quick schemes and too-good-to-be-true opportunities that can send you down a dangerous path.

The good news is that there are principles and strategies that can help anyone build and preserve wealth over the long term. And the earlier you start putting these into practice, the better your chances of success.

Below, I have mapped out some of the key principles of creating wealth, based on the web search results from Bing1234. I have also added some examples and tips to illustrate each principle.

PRINCIPLES OF CREATING WEALTH
1. Earn Money

The first thing you need to do is start making money. This step may seem elementary but is the most fundamental one for those who are just starting out.

• • •
137

You've probably seen charts showing that a small amount of money regularly saved and allowed to compound over time eventually can grow into a substantial sum. But those charts never answer this basic question: How do you get money to save in the first place?

There are two basic ways of making money: through earned income or passive income. Earned income comes from what you do for a living, while e passive income is derived from investments. You may not have any passive income until you've earned enough money to begin investing.

If you are either about to start a career or contemplating a career change, these questions may help you decide on what you want to do—and where your earned income is going to come from:

• What do you enjoy? You will perform better, build a longer-lasting career, and be more likely to succeed financially by doing something that you enjoy and find meaningful.

•   What are you good at? Look at what you do well and how you can use those talents to earn a living.

•   What will pay well? Look at careers using what you enjoy and doing well that will meet your financial expectations.

One good source of salary information, as well as the growth prospects for various fields, is the annual Occupational Outlook Handbook published by the U.S. Bureau of Labor Statistics.

Example: Alice loves writing and is good at creating engaging content. She decides to pursue a career as a freelance copywriter, where she can earn money by writing for different clients and projects. She researches the average rates and demand for copywriters in her niche and sets her fees accordingly.

Tip: To increase your earning potential, you can invest in your education and skills, seek opportunities for advancement, negotiate your salary, or create multiple streams of income.

2. Set Goals and Develop a Plan

What will you use your wealth for? Do you want to fund your retirement—maybe even an early one? Do you want to travel the world? Do you want to buy your dream home? Do you want to support a cause that you care about? Having a clear vision of what you want to achieve with your money will help you stay motivated and focused on your goal.

Once you have a goal in mind, you need to develop a plan to reach it. A good plan will include the following elements:

• A specific and measurable outcome. For example, instead of saying "I want to retire early", you can say "I want to retire at age 50 with $2 million in my portfolio".

• A realistic and attainable timeline. For example, instead of saying "I want to save $10,000 in a year", you can say "I want to save $10,000 in 3 years by saving $278 per month".

• A budget and a savings rate. A budget is a tool that helps you track your income and expenses and identify areas where you can save more or spend less. A savings rate is the percentage of your income that you save for your goal. For example, if you earn $5,000 per month and save $1,000, your savings rate is 20%.

• A strategy and a system. A strategy is a method that you use to grow your money, such as investing in the stock market, real estate, or a business. A system is a set of rules and habits that you follow to implement your strategy, such as automating your savings, diversifying your portfolio, or reinvesting your profits.

Example: Bob wants to travel the world for a year. He estimates that he will need $30,000 to cover his expenses. He sets a goal to save $30,000 in 5 years by saving $500 per month. He creates a budget to track his income and expenses and finds ways to reduce his spending and increase his income. He sets up a separate savings account for his travel fund and automates his monthly transfers. He also invests his savings in a diversified portfolio of low-cost index funds that match his risk tolerance and time horizon.

Tip: To make your plan more effective, you can review your progress regularly, adjust your plan as needed, and celebrate your milestones.

3. Save Money

Simply making money is not enough to build wealth. You also need to save money. Saving money means keeping some of your income for future use, rather than spending it all. Saving money allows you to:

•   Accumulate capital that you can invest to generate passive income and grow your wealth.

•   Build an emergency fund that can cover unexpected expenses or income loss and protect you from going into debt.

• Achieve your financial goals, such as buying a house, paying for education, or retiring comfortably.

The amount of money that you save depends on your income, expenses, and goals. A common rule of thumb is to save at least 10% of your income, but you can aim for a higher percentage if you want to achieve your goals faster or have a higher margin of safety.

Example: Charlie earns $4,000 per month and spends $3,000 on his living expenses. He saves $400 (10%) for his retirement fund, $200 (5%) for his emergency fund, and $200 (5%) for his vacation fund. He has a total savings rate of 20%.

Tip: To save more money, you can use the following strategies:

• Pay yourself first. This means setting aside a portion of your income for your savings before you spend anything else. You can do this by automating your transfers to your savings accounts or investment accounts.

• Spend less than you earn. This means living within your means and avoiding unnecessary or excessive spending. You can do this by creating and following a budget, using cash or debit cards instead of credit cards, and comparing prices before you buy.

• Increase your income. This means finding ways to earn more money, such as asking for a raise, getting a side hustle, or selling your unwanted items. You can do this by leveraging your skills, talents, and passions, and by networking and marketing yourself.

4. Invest Money

Saving money is not enough to build wealth. You also need to invest money. Investing money means putting your money to work for you, rather than letting it sit idle in a bank account. Investing money allows you to:

• Earn passive income from interest, dividends, or capital gains, without having to work for it.

• Beat inflation, which is the rise in the general level of prices over time, and which erodes the purchasing power of your money.

• Compound your money, which is the process of earning interest on your interest, and which accelerates the growth of your money over time.

The amount of money that you invest depends on your risk tolerance, time horizon, and goals. A common rule of thumb is to invest as much as you can, as early as you can, and as often as you can, while keeping some cash reserves for emergencies and opportunities.

Example: Diana has $10,000 in her savings account, earning 1% interest per year. She decides to invest $8,000 in a diversified portfolio of stocks and bonds, earning 8% interest per year, and keep $2,000 in her savings account for emergencies. After 10 years, her savings account will grow to $2,200, while her investment account will grow to $17,200.

Tip: To invest wisely, you can use the following strategies:

• Learn the basics of investing, such as the different types of assets, the relationship between risk and return, and the importance of diversification.

• Choose an investment strategy that suits your personality, goals, and resources, such as value investing, growth investing, or passive investing.

• Follow a proven investment system, such as the Wealth Within Trading System, that can help you identify, analyze, and execute profitable trades in the stock market.

5. Protect Money

Building wealth is not only about making, saving, and investing money. It is also about protecting money. Protecting money means safeguarding your money from potential threats, such as:

• Taxes, which are the compulsory contributions that you pay to the government, and which reduce your net income and returns.

•   Fees, which are the charges that you pay to various service providers, such as banks, brokers, or advisors, and which reduce your savings and returns.

•   Inflation, which is the rise in the general level of prices over time, and which erodes the purchasing power of your money.

•   Losses, which are the decreases in the value of your money due to market fluctuations, bad decisions, or unforeseen events.

•   Lawsuits, which are the legal actions that other parties may take against you, and which may result in financial liabilities or damages.

•   Theft, which is the act of taking your money without your consent, and which may result in financial losses or identity fraud.

The amount of money that you protect depends on your income, assets, and liabilities. A common

Besides the principles of creating wealth that I have already explained, there are some other principles that you may find useful, based on the web search results from Bing123. Here are some of them:

6. Manage Debt

Debt is a tool that can either help or hurt your wealth building process. It can help you by allowing you to leverage other people's money to buy assets that appreciate in value, such as a house or a business. It can hurt you by charging you interest and fees that eat away at your income and savings, especially if you use it to buy liabilities that depreciate in value, such as a car or a vacation.

The key to managing debt is to use it wisely and responsibly. You want to avoid or minimize high-interest debt, such as credit cards, payday loans, or personal loans, that can quickly spiral out of control and damage your credit score. You also want to pay off your debt as soon as possible, or at least make more than the minimum payments, to reduce the total amount of interest you pay overtime.

Example: Emma has $5,000 in credit card debt, with an interest rate of 18% per year. She decides to pay off her debt as fast as she can, by paying $500 per month. It will take her 12 months to pay off her debt, and she will pay $583 in interest. If she only paid the minimum payment of $100 per month, it would take her 94 months to pay off her debt, and she would pay $4,313 in interest.

Tip: To manage your debt better, you can use the following strategies:

•   Make a list of all your debts, including the balance, interest rate, and minimum payment for each one.

•   Choose a debt repayment method, such as the debt snowball or the debt avalanche, that suits your preference and motivation.

•   Consolidate your debt, if possible, by transferring your balances to a lower-interest loan or credit card, or by using a balance transfer offer.

•   Negotiate with your creditors, if necessary, to lower your interest rate, waive fees, or modify your payment plan.

7. Understand the Impact of Taxes

Taxes are a fact of life that you can't ignore or avoid. They are the compulsory contributions that you pay to the government, and they reduce your net income and returns. Taxes can have a significant impact on your wealth building process, depending on how much you earn, where you live, and how you invest.

The key to understanding the impact of taxes is to be aware of the different types of taxes that you may face, and how they affect your income and assets. You want to minimize your tax liability, or the amount of taxes that you owe, by taking advantage of the tax deductions, credits, and exemptions that you are eligible for. You also want to optimize your tax efficiency, or the ratio of after-tax returns to pre-tax returns, by choosing the appropriate tax-advantaged accounts and investments for your goals.

Example: Frank earns $100,000 per year and lives in California. He pays $24,000 in federal income tax, $9,300 in state income tax, and $7,650 in payroll tax, for a total tax liability of $40,950. His effective tax rate, or the percentage of his income that he pays in taxes, is 40.95%. He decides to contribute $19,500 to his 401(k) plan, which reduces his taxable income by the same amount. His new tax liability is $32,175, and his new effective tax rate is 32.18%. He also invests his 401(k) funds in a low-cost index fund, which has a low turnover rate and generates minimal capital gains and dividends, which are not taxed until he withdraws them.

Tip: To understand the impact of taxes better, you can use the following strategies:

•   Learn the basics of taxation, such as the different types of taxes, the tax brackets and rates, and the tax forms and deadlines.

•   Consult a tax professional, such as a certified public accountant (CPA) or an enrolled agent (EA), who can help you prepare your tax return, plan your tax strategy, and resolve any tax issues.

•   Use a tax software, such as TurboTax or H&R Block, that can help you file your taxes online, calculate your tax liability, and maximize your tax refund.

8. Build a Strong Credit History

Credit is a measure of your trustworthiness and ability to repay money that you borrow. Credit history is a record of your past and current credit activities, such as the types of credit you have, the amount of credit you use, and the timeliness of your payments. Credit score is a numerical representation of your credit history, ranging from 300 to 850, that lenders use to evaluate your creditworthiness and offer you interest rates and terms.

Credit can have a positive or negative impact on your wealth building process, depending on how you use it and manage it. Credit can help you by allowing you to access more money and opportunities, such as buying a house, starting a business, or getting a better job. Credit can hurt you by costing you more money and limiting your options, such as paying higher interest rates, fees, and penalties, or being denied credit, insurance, or employment.

The key to building a strong credit history is to use credit responsibly and maintain good credit habits. You want to establish and maintain a good credit score, or a score above 700, that reflects your creditworthiness and qualifies you for the best rates and terms. You also want to monitor and protect your credit history and score, by checking your credit reports regularly, disputing any errors, and preventing any fraud or identity theft.

Example: Grace has no credit history, as she has never used any credit products before. She decides to build her credit history by applying for a secured credit card, which requires a deposit as collateral. She uses her credit card for small purchases that she can afford to pay off in full every month, and never misses a payment.

She also signs up for a free credit monitoring service, such as Credit Karma or Credit Sesame, that tracks her credit score and alerts her of any changes or issues. After six months, she has a credit score of 720, and she qualifies for an unsecured credit card with a higher credit limit and lower interest rate.

Tip: To build a strong credit history, you can use the following strategies:

• Apply for and use credit products that suit your needs and goals, such as credit cards, loans, or lines of credit.

• Pay your bills on time and in full, or at least make more than the minimum payments, to avoid late fees, interest charges, and negative marks on your credit report.

• Keep your credit utilization ratio, or the percentage of your available credit that you use, below 30%, to show that you can manage your credit well.

• Mix your credit types, or the variety of credit products that you have, such as revolving credit (credit cards) and instalment credit (loans), to show that you can handle different kinds of credit.

A wealthy mindset is a set of beliefs, habits, and behaviors that separates the wealthy from the rest. A wealthy mindset will guide you to make the most of the money you have, and to find ways to increase your income and assets.

According to the web search results from Bing1234, some of the habits and skills that may help you cultivate a wealthy mindset are:

• Setting clear and realistic financial goals and developing a plan to achieve them.

• Saving and investing a portion of your income regularly and using compound interest to grow your wealth.

•   Seeking opportunities to earn more money, such as asking for a raise, starting a side hustle, or creating multiple streams of income.

•   Spending less than you earn and avoiding unnecessary or excessive spending on things that do not add value to your life.

•   Learning the basics of investing and choosing a strategy and a system that suit your personality, goals, and resources.

•   Managing your debt wisely and paying off high-interest debt as soon as possible.

•   Understanding the impact of taxes on your income and assets and minimizing your tax liability by taking advantage of deductions, credits, and exemptions.

•   Building a strong credit history and score and using credit responsibly and strategically.

•   Avoiding people who lack ambition, motivation, or positive attitude, and surrounding yourself with people who inspire, support, and challenge you.

- Maintaining a positive and optimistic outlook and believing in your ability to achieve your goals.

These habits and skills are not exclusive to the wealthy, and anyone can adopt them with some effort and discipline. By developing a wealthy mindset, you can improve your financial situation and well-being.

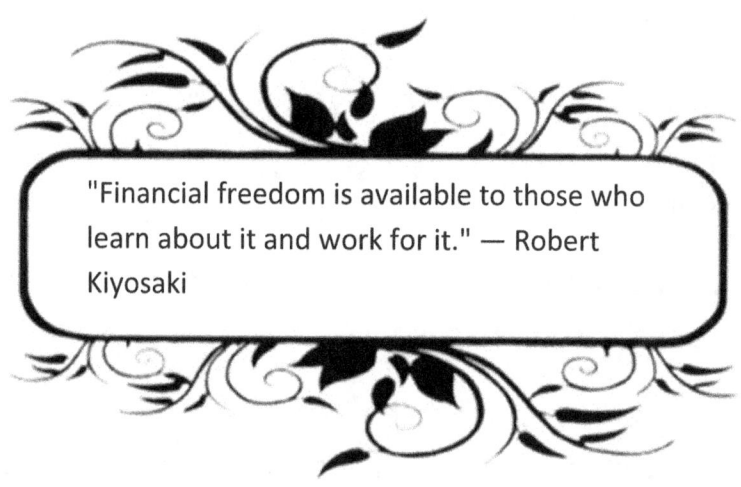

"Financial freedom is available to those who learn about it and work for it." — Robert Kiyosaki

CHAPTER NINE

WEALTHY MINDSET AND RELATIONSHIPS

Having a wealthy mindset can lead to living a fulfilled life in terms of relationships, because it can help you to:

• Appreciate the value of people, not just money. A wealthy mindset seeks to build relationships based on trust, shared values, and mutual respect. People with a wealthy mindset help others and cultivate relationships without expecting anything in return. A poor mindset thinks, "I scratch your back, you scratch mine."

• Communicate your needs and expectations clearly. A wealthy mindset allows you to express your financial goals and plans with your partner, family, and friends, and to seek their support and feedback. A poor mindset hides or lies about money matters or avoids talking about them altogether.

• Manage conflicts and disagreements constructively. A wealthy mindset enables you to handle money-related issues with empathy, compassion, and compromise. A poor mindset leads to resentment, blame, and hostility.

• Share your wealth and happiness with others. A wealthy mindset inspires you to give back to your community, donate to causes you care about, and celebrate your achievements with your loved ones. A poor mindset hoards money, envies others' success, and feels insecure or inadequate.

Therefore, having a wealthy mindset can improve your emotional and social well-being, and enhance the quality of your relationships.

Balancing your financial goals and your family responsibilities can be a challenging task, but it is not impossible. Here are some tips that may help you achieve a better balance:

• Communicate with your family members about your financial goals and plans and seek their support and feedback. You can also involve them in the budgeting and saving process and make it a fun and rewarding activity.

• Prioritize your financial goals and family responsibilities and allocate your time and resources accordingly. You may need to make some trade-offs and compromises but try to find a balance that works for you and your family.

• Use flexible work arrangements, if possible, to adjust your work hours or location to better suit your family needs. You can also ask your employer for other benefits or policies that can support your work-life balance, such as paid leave, childcare assistance, or wellness programs.

• Seek help from professional or personal caregivers, such as nannies, babysitters, relatives, or friends, to take care of your children or other dependents when you are busy with work or other obligations. You can also share your responsibilities with your partner or spouse and divide the tasks according to your strengths and preferences.

• Set boundaries between your work and family life and avoid mixing them unnecessarily. For example, you can turn off your work phone or email when you are spending time with your family and avoid bringing your family issues to work.

• Take care of yourself, and make time for your own hobbies, interests, and well-being. You can also spend quality time with your family and enjoy some fun and relaxing activities together. This can help you reduce stress, improve your mood, and strengthen your relationships.

Some Common Financial Challenges That Families Face Are:

•   Not enough income: Many families struggle to make ends meet with their current income, especially if they have been affected by the pandemic, layoffs, or pay cuts. They may need to find ways to increase their income, such as asking for a raise, getting a side hustle, or starting a business.

•   Too much debt: Many families have accumulated various types of debt, such as mortgage loans, auto loans, student loans, credit cards, or personal loans2. They may need to pay off their debt as soon as possible, or at least make more than the minimum payments, to reduce the interest charges and free up their cash flow3.

•   Lack of savings: Many families do not have enough savings to cover unexpected expenses, emergencies, or long-term goals, such as buying a house, paying for education, or retiring comfortably12. They may need to save more money, or at least 10% of their income, by creating and following a budget, spending less than they earn, and automating their savings.

•   High cost of living: Many families live in areas where the cost of living is high, such as housing, food, transportation, utilities, or taxes. They may need to relocate to a more affordable area, or find ways to reduce their expenses, such as comparing prices, using coupons, or sharing resources.

• Healthcare costs: Many families face high healthcare costs, either because they are uninsured, underinsured, or have a chronic or serious illness. They may need to get adequate health insurance, or shop around for the best rates and plans, and take care of their health by eating well, exercising, and avoiding bad habits3.

These are some of the financial challenges that families may face, but they are not insurmountable. With proper planning, budgeting, and discipline, families can overcome these challenges and achieve their financial goals.

Educating your children about wealthy mindset is a great way to help them develop positive and healthy attitudes towards money and wealth. A wealthy mindset is a set of beliefs, habits, and behaviors that can help anyone achieve their financial goals and live a fulfilling life.

According to the web search results from Bing1234, some of the ways you can educate your children about wealthy mindset are:

• Talk to them about money from an early age and use everyday situations as teachable moments. You can explain to them the basics of money, such as how it is earned, saved, spent, and invested, and how it can be used for good purposes, such as helping others or pursuing your passions.

• Give them an allowance and teach them how to manage it. You can encourage them to divide their allowance into jars or envelopes for saving, spending, and giving, and to set goals for each category. You can also help them track their progress and celebrate their achievements.

• Involve them in your family's financial decisions and plans. You can share with them your income and expenses, your budget and savings, and your financial goals and strategies. You can also ask for their opinions and suggestions, and let them participate in some of the choices, such as planning a vacation or buying a gift.

• Model good financial behavior and mindset. You can show them how you make, save, and invest your money, and how you deal with financial challenges and opportunities. You can also demonstrate positive and optimistic attitudes towards money, and avoid negative or limiting beliefs, such as money is scarce, hard to get, or evil.

• Encourage them to learn more about money and wealth. You can provide them with books, games, apps, or websites that can teach them more about financial literacy and skills. You can also introduce them to successful and inspiring people who have a wealthy mindset, such as entrepreneurs, investors, or philanthropists.

These are some of the ways you can educate your children about the wealthy mindset, but there are many more. The most important thing is to make it fun and engaging, and to tailor it to your children's age, interest, and personality. By doing so, you can help them develop a wealthy mindset that will serve them well throughout their lives.

Teaching your children about charity and giving back is a wonderful way to help them develop a generous and compassionate spirit. It can also benefit their personal growth, social responsibility, and emotional well-being.

There are many ways you can teach your children about charity and giving back, depending on their age, interest, and personality. Here are some general tips that may help you:

•   Talk to them about the meaning and importance of charity, and how it can make a positive difference in the world. You can use stories, books, videos, or examples from your own life to illustrate the concept of charity and its impact.

•   Give them an allowance and teach them how to manage it. You can encourage them to divide their allowance into three parts: saving, spending, and giving. You can also help them set goals for each part and track their progress.

•   Involve them in your family's charitable activities and decisions. You can share with them your family's values and causes and ask for their opinions and suggestions. You can also let them participate in some of the actions, such as donating money, goods, or time to a charity of their choice.

•   Expose them to different charitable causes and organizations and let them choose their own. You can research and discuss various issues and needs in your community and the world and find out what they are passionate about. You can also use online tools, such as Giving Assistant or The Giving Machine, to discover and support different charities.

• Make it fun and rewarding. You can use games, crafts, or parties to make charity more engaging and enjoyable for your children. You can also celebrate their achievements and efforts and praise their generosity and kindness.

These are some of the ways you can teach your children about charity and giving back, but there are many more. The most important thing is to make it a regular and consistent part of your family's life, and to model the behavior and mindset that you want your children to learn. By doing so, you can help your children develop a wealthy mindset that will serve them well throughout their lives.

RECOMMENDATION: I recommend some books and movies that can help you develop a wealthy mindset. A wealthy mindset is a set of beliefs, habits, and behaviors that can help you achieve your financial goals and live a fulfilling life.

According to the web search results from Bing1234, some of the best books and movies for wealthy mindset are:

• Mindset: The New Psychology of Success by Carol Dweck. This book is based on decades of research on how people's mindsets affect their performance and success. It shows how you can adopt a growth mindset that embraces challenges, learns from failures, and seeks improvement.

• The Wolf of Wall Street (2013). This movie is based on the true story of Jordan Belfort, who rose from a penny stockbroker to a wealthy and notorious Wall Street trader. It depicts his lavish and reckless lifestyle, as well as his downfall due to fraud and corruption.

• The Power of Broke by Daymond John. This book is written by the founder of FUBU and a Shark Tank investor, who started his clothing brand with a $40 budget. It shows how having limited resources can be an advantage, and how you can use your creativity, passion, and hustle to succeed.

• The Big Short (2015). This movie is based on the book by Michael Lewis, who chronicled the 2008 financial crisis and the people who predicted and profited from it. It exposes the flaws and corruption of the mortgage market, and the consequences of the collapse.

•   The Richest Man in Babylon by George Clason. This book is a classic that teaches the timeless principles of wealth creation and preservation. It uses stories and parables from ancient Babylon to illustrate the importance of saving, investing, and avoiding debt.

These are some of the books and movies that I recommend for wealthy mindset, but there are many more. You can find more suggestions by using the related searches from Bing, such as "best books on wealth creation" or "best movies about money and success". I hope you enjoy them and learn something valuable from them.

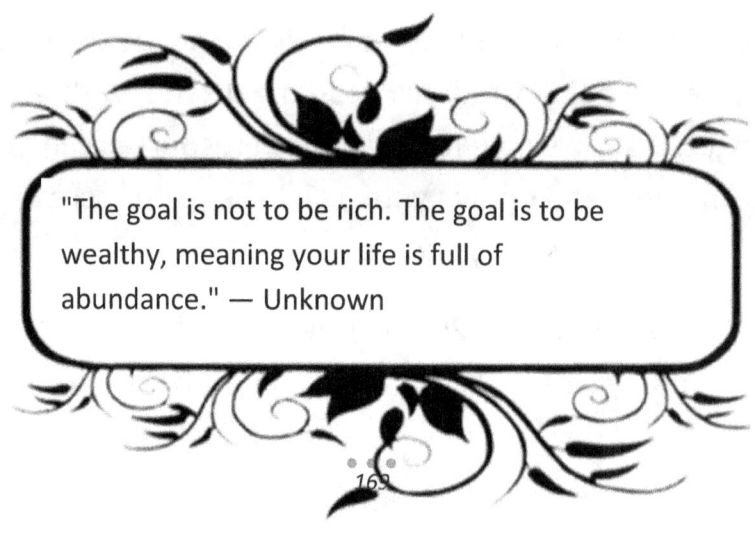

"The goal is not to be rich. The goal is to be wealthy, meaning your life is full of abundance." — Unknown

CHAPTER TEN

THE GLOSSARIES OF WEALTH CREATION

Here are some of the glossaries of wealth creation:

• Wealth Creation: The process of investing your saved money to grow your wealth by choosing investments that align with your financial goals.

• Compounding: The ability of an asset to generate earnings, which are then reinvested in order to generate their own earnings. In other words, compounding refers to generating earnings from previous earnings.

• Property Rights: The legal rights that an individual or a business has to use, control, and dispose of their property. Property rights are essential for wealth creation, as they provide incentives for people to invest, innovate, and trade.

• Division of Labour: The specialization of different individuals or groups in different tasks, with the aim of increasing productivity and efficiency. Division of labour is one of the factors that enables wealth creation, as it allows for greater output and quality of goods and services.

• SaaS: Software as a service, a business model where software is delivered over the internet and accessed by users on a subscription or pay-per-use basis. SaaS is a popular way of creating wealth in the digital economy, as it offers scalability, flexibility, and recurring revenue.

Yes, there are more glossaries of wealth creation that I found on the web. Here are some of them:

•   Asset Allocation: The process of dividing your investment portfolio among different asset classes, such as stocks, bonds, cash, and alternatives, to optimize your risk and return based on your goals, time horizon, and risk tolerance1.

•   Diversification: The strategy of investing in a variety of assets, sectors, markets, or strategies, to reduce the overall risk and volatility of your portfolio, and to increase the potential for higher returns.

•   Passive Income: The income that you earn without active involvement or work, such as interest, dividends, rent, royalties, or capital gains. Passive income can help you create wealth by providing a steady and consistent source of income, and by allowing you to reinvest your earnings and benefit from compounding3.

• Net Worth: The difference between your total assets and your total liabilities. Net worth is a measure of your financial health and wealth, and it can help you track your progress and evaluate your financial situation4.

• Financial Freedom: The state of having enough income and wealth to cover your living expenses and desired lifestyle, without having to work or depend on others. Financial freedom can give you more choices, opportunities, and happiness in life.

I hope this helps you understand the write-up better.

1: Asset Allocation Definition 2: Diversification Definition 3: Passive Income: What It Is and Why You Want It 4: Net Worth Definition 5: What is Financial Freedom? - Definition, Meaning & Examples

A CONCISE BOOK MAP FOR MY BOOK

Introduction:

Define the wealthy mindset and its significance.

Contrast it with poor and rich mindsets.

Principles of Wealthy Mindset:

Explore key principles (e.g., abundance, growth, resilience).

Explain how they shape financial decisions.

Habits for Wealth Building:

Discuss practical habits (e.g., budgeting, saving, investing).

Emphasize consistency and discipline.

Skills for Financial Success:

Cover essential skills (e.g., financial literacy, negotiation).

Provide actionable steps to acquire them.

Avoiding Common Pitfalls:

Identify mistakes people make (e.g., overspending, lack of planning).

Offer strategies to overcome challenges.

Achieving Financial Goals:

Detailed guidance on setting clear goals.

Techniques for achieving them confidently.

Effective Money Management:

Stress-free approaches to handling finances.

Tips for efficient money management.

Wealth Growth Strategies:

Leverage compounding, investments, and entrepreneurship.

Foster exponential wealth growth.

Wealth Protection and Enjoyment:

Safeguard wealth from risks (inflation, taxes, scams).

Cultivate guilt-free enjoyment of wealth.

Generosity and Impact:

Wise sharing of wealth with loved ones and causes.

Encourage positive impact.